Longman Pocket Companion Series

# Pocket Companion

# Contradictory Quotations

*This book was compiled and*
*edited by Hearn Stephenson*
*Publishing Limited*
*Published by*
**Longman Group Limited,**
*Longman House, Burnt Mill, Harlow,*
*Essex CM20 2JE, England*
*and Associated Companies throughout the world.*

© Longman Group Limited 1983


First published 1983

*British Library Cataloguing in Publication Data*
    Contradictory quotations.
    (Longman pocket companion series)
    1. Quotations, English
    I. Rogers, Michael, 1946–
    080      PN 6081
    ISBN 0–582–55698–8

Set in Monotype Photina


Printed and bound in Great Britain by
William Clowes (Beccles) Limited, Beccles and London

# Foreword

'I dogmatise and am contradicted, and in this
conflict of opinion and sentiments I find delight.'
Samuel Johnson

*Contradictory Quotations* is an anthology of logger-
headed opinions, verbal punches and counter-
punches, conversational opening shots and return
fire, argumentative thrusts and parries, all
arranged to illustrate one immutable law: for
every Truth wittily expressed there is an opposite
and equal Truth. If this is the First Law of Good
Conversation, the Second inevitably contradicts it.

This pocket-sized selection of statements and
counter-statements is, of necessity, somewhat
arbitrary and personal and readers may – I hope –
feel outraged from time to time that *their* favourite
quotations have been omitted. I can only plead, as
did that other and most illustrious 'harmless
drudge', that it was due to 'ignorance . . . pure
ignorance'. After all, this book is *about*
disagreement and if it stimulates people to play
their own game of literary Pelmanism, so much
the better.

Covering a fairly wide span of those topics about
which people never-failingly argue, *Contradictory
Quotations* celebrates some of those precious vices
which make for good, entertaining and
stimulating debate: contrariness, combativeness
and contradiction, bloody-mindedness and
pugnacity and, of course, the love of argument for
its own sake – here the means are the end. In fact it
is a little handbook for Devil's Advocates and is
dedicated to all those who answer back.

Above all, these confrontations are meant to act as
antidotes to aphorism. The aphorist (aphorizer in
American, *aphoriviste* or nouveau-bore in French)
is the deadly enemy of good talk. Aphorists are
wise with the miniaturized wisdom of the
Christmas cracker motto and smugly sage with the
freeze-dried sagacity of fortune cookies.

Special thanks are due to Judith Harris, Anne
Stephenson, Tom Taussik, Stelios Galatopoulos
and Nina Kent, and to Alan Hamp for designing
this book.
Michael Rogers

The movie actor, like the sacred king of primitive tribes, is a god in captivity.
ALEXANDER CHASE
*Perspectives*, 1966

I think the whole business of being an actor and being part of entertainment, whether it be TV shows or stage shows or movies, is noble.
WALTER MATTHAU, 1979

Acting is a matter of calculated instinct.
ERNEST BORGNINE

The real actor – like any real artist – has a direct line to the collective heart.
BETTE DAVIS

Acting is the expression of a neurotic impulse.
MARLON BRANDO

Each time an actor acts he does not hide; he exposes himself.
JEANNE MOREAU, 1976

Only a true actor with a deep-seated compulsion is going to stick out the struggle that goes with being in the theater. It's brutal, it's worse than a marine boot camp . . . .
HELEN HAYES

God makes stars.
SAM GOLDWYN

Don't act – think!
F. W. MURNAU

She knows the world, but this knowledge has not lowered her great and benevolent dignity; its darkness has not dimmed her goodness.
EDITH SITWELL, on Marilyn Monroe

Actors are crap.

JOHN FORD

Actors are cattle.

ALFRED HITCHCOCK

Learn the lines and don't bump into the furniture.

NOËL COWARD (attrib.)

Players, Sir! I look on them as no better than creatures set upon tables and joint stools to make faces and produce laughter, like dancing dogs.

SAMUEL JOHNSON
in Boswell, *Life of Johnson*, 1791

The better the actor the more stupid he is.

TRUMAN CAPOTE

Being another character is more interesting than being yourself.

SIR JOHN GIELGUD

I think the theatre is a wonderful holiday . . .

TONY RICHARDSON, 1966

With me it was 5 percent talent and 95 percent publicity.

MARION DAVIES

I am paid not to think.

CLARK GABLE

Like kissing Hitler.

TONY CURTIS, on Marilyn Monroe

I wasn't cut out to be an actor. I haven't the
energy for acting – it's too exhausting.
LESLEY HOWARD

The important thing for a star is to have an
interesting face. He doesn't have to move it very
much. Editing and camerawork can always
produce the desired illusion.
GEORGE SANDERS

I love every aspect of motion pictures and I guess I
am committed to it for life.
CLINT EASTWOOD

She makes dialog sound better than it is by a
matchless clarity and beauty of diction and by a
fineness of intelligence and sensibility that
illuminates every shade of meaning in every line
she speaks.
TENNESSEE WILLIAMS, on Katherine Hepburn

I really believe in the work effort. I like people who
work on things.
DIANE KEATON

The physical labor actors have to do wouldn't tax
an embryo.

SPENCER TRACY

I am the unusual and do not need camera angles.

CHARLIE CHAPLIN

Acting is a bum's life. Quitting acting, that is a sign
of maturity.

MARLON BRANDO

She ran the whole gamut of emotions from A to B.

DOROTHY PARKER, on Katherine Hepburn

Anyone who works is a fool. I don't work – I
merely inflict myself on the public.

ROBERT MORLEY

I look forward to a great future for America – a future in which our country will match its military strength with our moral restraint, its wealth with our wisdom, its power with our purpose.
JOHN F. KENNEDY, 1963

The great and admirable strength of America consists in this, that America is truly the American people.
JACQUES MARITAIN

From the very beginning our people have markedly combined practical capacity for affairs with power of devotion to an ideal.
THEODORE ROOSEVELT, 1902

America was not established to create wealth but to realize a vision, to realize an ideal – to discover and maintain liberty among men.
WOODROW WILSON, 1912

Give me your tired, your poor, / Your huddled masses yearning to be free.
EMMA LAZARUS, 1849–1887

Chicago has a strange metaphysical elegance of death about it.
CLAES OLDENBURG

. . . a city rich and vigorous and full of pride, a city lost and beaten and full of emptiness.
RAYMOND CHANDLER, on Los Angeles

A thousand years hence, perhaps in less, America may be what Europe is now . . . the noblest work of human wisdom, the grand scene of human glory.
THOMAS PAINE

# America & Americans

The organization of American society is an
interlocking system of semi-monopolies
notoriously venal, an electorate notoriously
unenlightened, misled by mass-media notoriously
phony.

PAUL GOODMAN
*The Community of Scholars*, 1962

The American people, taking one with another,
constitute the most sniveling, poltroonish,
ignominious mob of serfs and goose-steppers ever
gathered under the flag in Christendom since the
end of the Middle Ages.

H. L. MENCKEN
*Prejudices*, 1922

There is nothing the matter with Americans
except their ideals.

G. K. CHESTERTON, 1931

With the supermarket as our temple and the
singing commercial as our litany, are we likely to
fire the world with an irresistable vision of
America's exalted purpose?

ADLAI STEVENSON, 1963

The worst country to be poor in is America.

ARNOLD TOYNBEE

This is virgin territory for whorehouses.

AL CAPONE, on suburban Chicago

The difference between Los Angeles and yogurt is
that yogurt has real culture.

TOM TAUSSIK
*Legless in Gaza*, 1982

I have seen the future and it does not work.

PHILIP TOYNBEE, 1974

# Animals

No bird sits a tree more proudly than a pigeon.
It looks as though placed there by the Lord.
KATHERINE MANSFIELD
*Journal*, 1922

If only men could love each other like dogs, the
world would be a paradise.
JAMES DOUGLAS

People who are anti-dog are anti-sex.
JILLY COOPER, 1977

Dogs live with man as courtiers round a monarch,
steeped in the flattery of his notice and enriched
with sinecures. To push their favour in this world
of pickings and caresses is, perhaps the business of
their lives . . . .
ROBERT LOUIS STEVENSON
*The Character of Dogs*, 1883

Of all God's creatures there is only one that cannot
be made the slave of the lash. That one is the cat. If
man could be crossed with the cat it would
improve man, but it would deteriorate the cat.
MARK TWAIN
*Notebook*, 1935

It is easy to understand why the rabble dislike cats.
BAUDELAIRE
*Mon coeur mis à nu*, 1887

Not the least hard thing to bear when they go from
us, these quiet friends, is that they carry away with
them so many years of our own lives.
GALSWORTHY, on dogs
*Memories*, 1914

... rats with wings.

WOODY ALLEN, on pigeons
*Stardust Memories*, 1980

It's the one species I wouldn't mind seeing vanish from the face of the earth. I wish they were like the White Rhino – six of them left in the Serengeti National Park, and all males.

ALAN BENNETT
*Getting On*, 1974

You will find that the woman who is really kind to dogs is always one who has failed to inspire sympathy in men.

MAX BEERBOHM
*Zuleika Dobson*, 1911

The best kind of dog is the hotdog, because it's the only dog that feeds the hand that bites it.

anon

One hell of a nice animal, frequently mistaken for a meatloaf.

B. KLIBAN

People with insufficient personalities are fond of cats. These people adore being ignored.

HENRY MORGAN

I loathe people who keep dogs. They are cowards who haven't got the guts to bite people themselves.

AUGUST STRINDBERG
*A Madman's Diary*

# Architecture

Good architecture is like a piece of beautifully
composed music crystallized in space that elevates
our spirits beyond the limitation of time.
TAO HO, 1980


Architecture is the total of man's man-made
physical surroundings. The only thing I leave out
is nature.
EERO SAARINEN, 1956


Shall we attempt to condense the central issue
facing architecture today into one sentence?
Colours which you can see with ears; sounds to
see with eyes; the void you touch with your
elbows; the taste of space on your tongue; the
fragrance of dimensions; the juice of stone.
MARCEL BREUER


The Gothic cathedral is a blossoming in stone
subdued by the insatiable demand of harmony in
man.
EMERSON
*Essays: First Series*, 1841


Less is more.
MIES VAN DER ROHE


When we build let us think that we build for
ever.
RUSKIN
*The Seven Lamps of Architecture*, 1849


Architecture is the will of an epoch translated into
space.
MIES VAN DER ROHE


In architecture . . . the *end* is to build well.
SIR HENRY WOTTON
*Elements of Architecture*, 1624

# Architecture

I don't believe that architecture is ennobling . . . to me it's merely a matter of kicks.

PHILIP JOHNSON, 1974

The materials of city planning are sky, space, trees, steel and cement in that order and in that hierarchy.

LE CORBUSIER

We should learn from the snail; it has devised a home that is both exquisite and functional.

FRANK LLOYD WRIGHT

. . . the Gothic is at once the most logical and the most beautiful. It reaches up magnificently – and a good half of it is palpably useless.

H. L. MENCKEN, 1931

Less is only more where more is no good.

FRANK LLOYD WRIGHT<br>The Future of Architecture, 1953

The genius of architecture seems to have shed its maledictions over this land.

THOMAS JEFFERSON<br>Notes on the State of Virginia, 1784–5

Architecture is the art of how to waste space.

PHILIP JOHNSON, 1964

To build is to be robbed.

SAMUEL JOHNSON<br>The Idler, 1758–60

What makes the artist is his power to shape the
material of pain we all have.
LIONEL TRILLING
*The Liberal Imagination*, 1950

Great art . . . is preeminently and finally the
expression of the spirits of great men.
RUSKIN
*Modern Painters*, 1843–60

No artist is ahead of his time. He *is* his time.
It is just that others are behind the time.
MARTHA GRAHAM

An artist conscientiously moves in a direction
which for some good reason he takes, putting one
work in front of the other with the hope he'll arrive
before death.
JOHN CAGE
*Silence*, 1961

One must have chaos in oneself to be able to give
birth to a dancing star.
NIETZSCHE
*Thus Spake Zarathustra*, 1883–92

The moment you cheat for the sake of beauty, you
know you are an artist.
MAX JACOB
*Art poétique*, 1922

The artist's egoism is outrageous: it must be; he is
by nature a solipsist and the world exists only for
him to exercise upon it his powers of creation.
W. SOMERSET MAUGHAM
*The Summing Up*, 1938

Only in men's imagination does every truth find an
effective and undeniable existence. Imagination,
not invention, is the supreme master of art as of
life.
JOSEPH CONRAD
*A Personal Record*, 1912

... the artist has an imperative need to make
others share the joy which he experiences himself.

IGOR STRAVINSKY
*An Autobiography*, 1936

The artist is not a special kind of man. Every man
is a special kind of artist.

ERIC GILL

An artist must be a reactionary.

EVELYN WAUGH

There is no progress in art.

ILYA EHRENBERG, 1967

The artistic temperament is a disease that afflicts
amateurs.

G. K. CHESTERTON
*Heretics*, 1905

Artists – by definition innocent – don't steal,
but do borrow without giving back.

NED ROREM
*Music From Inside Out*, 1967

The world of sight is still limitless. It is the artist
who limits vision to the cramped dimension of his
own ego.

MARYA MANNES
*More in Anger*, 1958

Imagination – it is that deceitful part in man, that
mistress of error and falsity ...

PASCAL
*Pensées*, 1670

Art is not a mirror to reflect the world, but a
hammer with which to shape it.
VLADIMIR MAYAKOVSKY

Art is the right hand of nature.
SCHILLER
*Fiesco*, 1783


Life is very nice, but it lacks form. It's the aim of art
to give it some.
JEAN ANOUILH
*The Rehearsal*, 1950


There is no comfort in adversity / More sweet than
Art affords.
AMPHIS, 4th century B.C.

All art is a kind of confession ... All artists, if they
are to survive, are forced, at last, to tell the whole
story, to vomit the anguish up.
JAMES BALDWIN
*Nobody Knows My Name*, 1961

Art is the expression of the profoundest thought in
the simplest way.
ALBERT EINSTEIN

Drawing is a way of reasoning on paper.
SAUL STEINBERG


All art is a fight against decay.
BRIAN ALDISS, 1971

Art never initiates. It merely takes over what is
already present in the real world and makes an
aesthetic pattern out of it, or tries to explain it, or
tries to relate it to some other aspect of life.
ANTHONY BURGESS, 1974

Artists are the unacknowledged legislators of the
world.
JONATHAN MILLER, 1964

Sculpture is not for young men.

CONSTANTIN BRANCUSI

The only domain where the divine is visible is that of art, whatever name we choose to call it.

ANDRÉ MALRAUX<br>*Les Métamorphoses des Dieux*, 1957

The attitude that nature is chaotic and that the artist puts order into it is a very absurd point of view, I think. All that we can hope for is to put some order into ourselves.

WILLIAM DE KOONING, 1951

Art is meant to disturb.

GEORGES BRAQUE

To reveal art and conceal the artist, is art's aim.

OSCAR WILDE<br>*The Picture of Dorian Gray*, 1891

Art is the sex of the imagination.

GEORGE JEAN NATHAN, 1926

When an artist reasons, it's because he no longer understands.

ANDRÉ DERAIN

A great work of art is a kind of suicide.

A. ALVAREZ, 1971

A work of art has no reference to anything outside itself.

ALAIN ROBBE-GRILLET, 1962

Art is the great refusal of the world as it is.

HERBERT MARCUSE

Poetry . . . takes its origin from emotion recollected
in tranquillity.
WORDSWORTH
Preface to the *Lyrical Ballads*

Art is one of the few things, apart from love and
friendship, to be worth caring about.
BRIAN ALDISS, 1971

All art deals with the absurd and aims at the
simple. Good art speaks truth, indeed *is* truth,
perhaps the only truth.
IRIS MURDOCH

Art is a vision of heaven gratuitously given.
ANTHONY BURGESS
1985, 1978

Art is as important as council housing.
ILLTYD HARRINGTON, 1975

The true work of art is one which the seventh
wave of genius throws up the beach where the
undertow of time cannot drag it back.
CYRIL CONNOLLY
*The Unquiet Grave*, 1945

Painting is a blind man's profession. He paints not
what he sees but what he feels, what he tells
himself about what he has seen.
PABLO PICASSO

An artist is only someone unrolling and digging
out and excavating the areas normally accessible
to normal people everywhere and exhibiting them
as a sort of scarecrow to show people what can be
done with themselves.
LAWRENCE DURRELL

Art is the most frenzied orgy a man is capable of.
JEAN DUBUFFET

In the end art is small beer. The really serious
things in life are earning one's living so as not to be
a parasite and loving one's neighbour.
W. H. AUDEN, 1970

Art is the lie that enables us to realize the truth.
PABLO PICASSO

Creativity is merely a plus name for regular
activity.

JOHN UPDIKE, 1968

A work of art has no importance whatever to
society. It is only important to the individual.
VLADIMIR NABOKOV
*Strong Opinions*, 1974

I think painting dies, you understand. After 40 or
50 years a picture dies because its freshness
disappears . . . I think a picture dies after a few
years like the man who painted it.
MARCEL DUCHAMP

Anyone who sees and paints a sky green and
pastures blue ought to be sterilized.
ADOLF HITLER

If it is art it is not for all and if it is for all it is not
art.
ARNOLD SCHOENBERG

# Beauty

The human soul needs actual beauty more than
bread.
D. H. LAWRENCE
*Assorted Articles*, 1930

Beauty is how you feel inside and it reflects in your
eyes. It is not something physical.
SOPHIA LOREN, 1978

The best thing is to look natural, but it takes
makeup to look natural.
CALVIN KLEIN, 1977

We fly to Beauty as an asylum from the terrors of
finite nature.
EMERSON
*Journals*, 1836

Any extraordinary degree of beauty in man or
woman involves a moral charm.
EMERSON
*The Conduct of Life*, 1860

A great nose indicates a great man – / Genial,
courteous, intellectual, / Virile, courageous.
EDMOND ROSTAND
*Cyrano de Bergerac*, 1879

A handsome man is not quite poor.
Spanish proverb

After a degree of prettiness, one pretty girl is as
pretty as another.
F. SCOTT FITZGERALD
"The Crack-Up", 1936

I think most of the beauty of women evaporates
when they achieve domestic happiness at the price
of their independence.
CYRIL CONNOLLY
*The Unquiet Grave*, 1944

Beauty does not season soup.

Polish proverb

A woman is truly beautiful only when she is naked and she knows it.

ANDRÉ COURRÈGES

Most women are not so young as they are painted.

MAX BEERBOHM<br>"In Defence of Cosmetics", 1922

There is nothing sane about the worship of beauty.

OSCAR WILDE<br>Intentions, 1891

Beauty is its own excuse for being.

EMERSON<br>May Day and Other Pieces, 1867

If the eyes are sometimes the organ through which our intelligence is revealed, the nose is generally the organ in which stupidity is most readily displayed.

MARCEL PROUST<br>Remembrance of Things Past: Cities of the Plain,<br>1913–27

Often a noble face hides filthy ways.

EURIPIDES<br>Electra, 413 B.C.

All heiresses are beautiful.

DRYDEN<br>King Arthur, 1695

My mother has witish yelow hare, pinkish eyes and lots of teeth and she is very butifull.

ANN<br>aged 6, in Lots of Love, compiled by Nanette<br>Newman, 1974

# Bloodsports

There is a passion for hunting something deeply
implanted in the human breast.
DICKENS
*Oliver Twist*, 1837–8


Shooting gives me a good feeling.
ERNEST HEMINGWAY
"Fathers and Sons", 1944


... the bullfight is very moral to me because I feel
very fine while it is going on and have a feeling of
life and death and immortality, and after it is over I
feel very sad but very fine.
ERNEST HEMINGWAY
*Death in the Afternoon*, 1932


Tell me a man's a fox-hunter, and I loves him at
once.
R. S. SURTEES
*Handley Cross*, 1843


Killing by itself is not the hunter's object. The very
people who shudder most over the cruelty of the
hunter are apt to forget that slaughter, in the
grimmest sense of the word, is a process that they
entrust daily to the butcher.
LEWIS MUMFORD
*Green Memories*, 1947


... the chase, the sport of kings / Images of war
without its guilt.
WILLIAM SOMERVILLE
"The Chase"

The human spirit sublimates / the impulses it
thwarts; / a healthy sex life mitigates / the lust for
other sports.

PIET HEIN
*Grooks*, 1966

... hatred, jealousy, boastfulness, disregard of all
rules and sadistic pleasure in witnessing violence.

GEORGE ORWELL
*Shooting an Elephant*, 1950

... there is surely nothing more beautiful in this
world than the sight of a lone man facing single
handedly a half a ton of angry pot roast.

TOM LEHRER
"In Old Mexico", 1959

No sportsman wants to kill the fox or the pheasant
as I want to kill him when I see him doing it.

GEORGE BERNARD SHAW

It is very strange and very melancholy, that the
paucity of human pleasures should persuade us
ever to call hunting one of them.

SAMUEL JOHNSON

The English country gentleman galloping after a
fox – the unspeakable in full pursuit of the
uneatable.

OSCAR WILDE
*A Woman of No Importance*, 1893

# Britain

Oh, to be in England / Now that April's there.
BROWNING
"Home Thoughts From Abroad"

England! awake! awake! awake! / Jerusalem thy
sister calls!
WILLIAM BLAKE
*Jerusalem*, 1804–20

England is the paradise of individuality,
eccentricity, heresy, anomalies, hobbies, and
humours.
GEORGE SANTAYANA
*Soliloquies in England*, 1922

Remember that you are an Englishman, and have
consequently won first prize in the lottery of life.
CECIL RHODES

The halesome parritch, chief of Scotia's food.
ROBERT BURNS
"The Cotter's Saturday Night"

O ye'll tak' the high road, and I'll tak' the low
road, / And I'll be in Scotland afore ye . . .
anon

You'll hear more wit, and better wit, in an Irish
street row than would keep Westminster Hall in
humour for five weeks.
WALTER BAGEHOT
*Literary Studies*, 1879

I must be permitted – I really must – to say a word
or two about the language . . . "Sweet Welsh".
GEORGE BORROW
*Wild Wales*, 1862

The climate of England has been the world's most
powerful colonizing impulse.

RUSSELL GREEN

The nobility of England, my lord, would have
snored through the Sermon on the Mount.

ROBERT BOLT
*A Man For All Seasons*, 1960

They are the most embarrassed people in this
world, the English.

ALAN BENNETT
*The Old Country*, 1978

In England, failure is all the rage.

QUENTIN CRISP
*The Naked Civil Servant*, 1968

*Oats.* A grain which in England is generally given
to horses, but in Scotland supports the people.

SAMUEL JOHNSON
*Dictionary*, 1755

Sir, the noblest prospect that a Scotchman ever
sees, is the high road that leads him to London.

SAMUEL JOHNSON
in Boswell, *Journal of a Tour to the Hebrides*, 1785

The problem with Ireland is that it's a country full
of genius, but with absolutely no talent.

HUGH LEONARD

Anyone who learns that bloody awful language,
Welsh, well enough to make a speech, deserves our
respect.

C. DAY LEWIS, on Prince Charles

# Capitalism

The moment the idea is admitted into society that property is not as sacred as the laws of God . . . anarchy and tyranny commence.
JOHN ADAMS

The growth of a large business is merely the survival of the fittest . . . The American Beauty rose can be produced in the splendor and fragrance which bring cheer to its beholder only by sacrificing the early buds which grow up around it.
JOHN D. ROCKEFELLER

Money-getters are the benefactors of our race. To them . . . we are indebted for our institutions of learning, and of art, our academies, colleges and churches.
PHINEAS T. BARNUM

Civilization and profits go hand in hand.
CALVIN COOLIDGE

A great society is a society in which men of business think greatly of their function.
ALFRED NORTH WHITEHEAD

Every great man of business has got somewhere a touch of the idealist in him.
WOODROW WILSON

The spirit of property doubles a man's strength.
VOLTAIRE
*Philosophical Dictionary*, 1764

The smell of profit is clean / And sweet, whatever the source.
JUVENAL
*Satires, c.* 100 A.D.

# Capitalism

We stand for the maintenance of private property.
ADOLF HITLER

Free enterprise ended in the United States a good
many years ago. Big oil, big steel, big agriculture
avoid the open market place. Big corporations fix
prices among themselves and drive out the small
entrepreneur. In their conglomerate forms, the
huge corporations have begun to challenge the
legitimacy of the State.

GORE VIDAL

You show me a capitalist, I'll show you a
bloodsucker.

MALCOLM X
*Malcolm X Speaks,* 1965

There is a good deal of solemn cant about the
common interests of capital and labor. As matters
stand, their only common interest is that of cutting
each other's throat.

BROOKS ATKINSON
*Once Around the Sun,* 1951

It is well known what a middle man is: he is a man
who bamboozles one party and plunders the other.
DISRAELI, 1845

Callous greed grows pious very fast.
LILLIAN HELLMAN

Property is theft.

PROUDHON
*Qu'est-ce que la propriété?,* 1840

What is a man if he is not a thief who openly
charges as much as he can for the goods he sells?
M. K. GANDHI
*Non-Violence in Peace and War,* 1948

# Certainty & Doubt

The art of living is the art of knowing how to
believe lies.
CESARE PAVESE

If the cause be good, the most violent attack of its
enemies will not injure it so much as an
injudicious defense of it by its friends.
CHARLES CALEB COLTON
*Lacon*, 1825

In a just cause the weak will beat the strong.
SOPHOCLES
*Oedipus at Colonus*, 401 B.C.

Doubt and mistrust are the mere panic of timid
imagination, which the steadfast heart will
conquer and the large mind transcend.
HELEN KELLER
*Optimism*, 1903

Faith, to my mind, is a stiffening process, a sort of
mental starch, which ought to be applied as
sparingly as possible.
E. M. FORSTER
*What I Believe*, 1951

Man is a fighting animal; his thoughts are his
banners, and it is a failure of nerve in him if they
are only thoughts.
GEORGE SANTAYANA
*Dialogues in Limbo*, 1925

It is only in the lonely emergencies of life that our
creed is tested: then routine maxims fail, and we
fall back on our gods.
WILLIAM JAMES
*The Will to Believe*, 1896

To have his path made clear for him is the
aspiration of every human being in our beclouded
and tempestuous existence.
JOSEPH CONRAD
*The Mirror of the Sea*, 1906

Doubt is not a pleasant mental state but certainty
is a ridiculous one.

VOLTAIRE

A just cause is not ruined by a few mistakes.

DOSTOEVSKY, 1895

It is characteristic of all movements and crusades
that the psychopathic element rises to the top.

ROBERT LINDNER
*Must You Conform?*, 1956

The quest for certainty blocks the search for
meaning. Uncertainty is the very condition to
impel man to unfold his powers.

ERICH FROMM
*Man for Himself*, 1947

Faith is much better than belief. Belief is when
someone *else* does the thinking.

R. BUCKMINSTER FULLER, 1972

General and abstract ideas are the source of the
greatest errors of mankind.

ROUSSEAU
*Emile*, 1762

I know that a creed is the shell of a lie.

AMY LOWELL
*What's O'Clock*, 1925

If you would be a real seeker after truth, it is
necessary that at least once in your life you doubt,
as far as possible, all things.

DESCARTES

# Children

Children are God's apostles, day by day / Sent forth to preach love, and hope, and peace.
JAMES RUSSELL LOWELL
"On the Death of a Friend's Child", 1844

Children are remarkable for their . . . intolerance of shams, the clarity and ruthlessness of their vision.
ALDOUS HUXLEY
*Music at Night*, 1931

If men do not keep on speaking terms with children, they cease to be men, and become merely machines for eating and for earning money.
JOHN UPDIKE
*Assorted Prose*, 1965

The truly passionate are little boys.
MURRAY KEMPTON
*America Comes of Middle Age*, 1963

A fairly bright boy is more intelligent and far better company than the average adult.
J. B. S. HALDANE, 1948

To an old father, nothing is more sweet / Than a daughter. Boys are more spirited but their ways / Are not so tender.
EURIPIDES
*The Suppliant Women*, c. 421 B.C.

The discontented child cries for toasted snow.
Arab proverb

Children are on a different plane, they belong to a generation and way of feeling properly their own.
GEORGE SANTAYANA

# Children

Children are completely egotistic; they feel their
needs intensely and strive ruthlessly to satisfy
them.

SIGMUND FREUD
*The Interpretation of Dreams*, 1899

Only those in the last stage of disease could believe
that children are true judges of character.

W. H. AUDEN
*The Orators*, 1932

Anybody who hates children and dogs can't be all
bad.

W. C. FIELDS (attrib.)

He who was first an acolyte, and afterwards an
abbot or curate, knows what the boys do behind
the altar.

Spanish proverb

Boys are capital fellows in their own way ... but
they are unwholesome companions for grown
people.

CHARLES LAMB
*Essays of Elia*, 1823

He who has daughters is always a shepherd.

Spanish proverb

If a child shows himself incorrigible, he should be
decently and quietly beheaded at the age of twelve.

DON MARQUIS
*The Almost Perfect State*, 1952

I do not believe in a child world ... I believe the
child should be taught from the very first that the
whole world is his world, that adult and child
share one world, that all generations are needed.

PEARL S. BUCK
*To My Daughters, With Love*, 1967

The best films are best because of nobody but the director.
ROMAN POLANSKI

A film is never really good unless the camera is an eye in the head of a poet.
ORSON WELLES

Anyone can direct a good picture if he's got a good script.
GARSON KANIN

I want to rule by love, not fear.
LOUIS B. MAYER

The cinema is truth 24 times a second.
JEAN-LUC GODARD

It's the kissiest business in the world. You *have* to keep kissing people . . .
AVA GARDNER

. . . there will always be difficulty if you have a creative producer unless there is tremendous teamwork.
STANLEY KRAMER

It's the biggest trainset a boy ever had.
ORSON WELLES, on Hollywood

A film director is not a creator, but a midwife. His business is to deliver the actor of a child that he did not know he had inside him.
JEAN RENOIR
*My Life and My Films*, 1974

Millions are to be grabbed out here and your only competition is idiots.
HERMAN MANKIEWITZ, describing the emergent Hollywood to Ben Hecht

On a film set the only person less important than a
director is a talent agent.

JOHN CASSAVETES

A good film is when the price of the dinner, the
theatre admission and the babysitter were worth
it.

ALFRED HITCHCOCK, 1960

I care nothing about the story, only how it is
photographed and presented.

JOSEF VON STERNBERG

The producer shouldn't get ulcers, he should give
them.

SAM GOLDWYN

The cinema is not a slice of life, it's a piece of cake.

ALFRED HITCHCOCK, 1960

Moving pictures is the cruelest business in the
world. You must be like a boxer all the time, with
your left hand out.

MIKE CURTIZ

A team effort is a lot of people doing what I say.

MICHAEL WINNER

Hollywood is a sewer – with service from the Ritz-
Carlton.

WILSON MIZNER

Ninety-five percent of films are born of frustration,
of self-despair, of poverty, of ambition for survival,
for money, for fattening bank accounts.

SAM FULLER

Hollywood money isn't money. It's congealed
snow, melts in your hand, and there you are.

DOROTHY PARKER

# The City

I have an affection for a great city. I feel safe in the
neighborhood of man, and enjoy the sweet
security of the streets.
LONGFELLOW
*Driftwood*, 1857

To say the least, a town life makes one more
tolerant and liberal in one's judgement of others.
LONGFELLOW
*Hyperion*, 1839

Miró breathes in the air. "Ah, what vitamins!
This city is a tonic! This city is a doctor!"
JOHN GRUEN
on Juan Miró in New York

There is something about an open fire, bread and
butter sandwiches, very strong tea, yellow fog
without and the cultural drawl of English voices
which makes London very attractive and if I had
been fascinated before, from that moment I loved it
dearly.
ISADORA DUNCAN
*My Life*, 1928

Only by returning to life in the city does one
rediscover the unbelievable complexity,
excitement, and beauty of the human face. There
are faces in the country, of course, but they are
widely spaced like filling stations.
JEROME WEIDMAN

The pleasure of being in crowds is a mysterious
expression of sensual joy in the multiplication of
Number.
BAUDELAIRE
*Mon coeur mis à nu*, 1887

A neighborhood is where, when you go out of it,
you get beat up.
Puerto Rican worker, quoted in
Kempton, *America Comes of Age*, 1963


In great cities men are more callous both to the
happiness and the misery of others ... for they are
constantly in the habit of seeing both extremes.

CHARLES CALEB COLTON
*Lacon*, 1825

As a city, New York moves in the forefront of
today's great trend of great cities toward neurosis.
She is confused, self-pitying, helpless and
dependent.

JOHN LARDNER, 1953

London seems to me like some hoary massive
underworld, a hoary ponderous inferno. The traffic
pours through the rigid grey streets like the rivers
of hell ...

D. H. LAWRENCE
*Selected Letters*, 1950

I'd rather wake up in the middle of nowhere than
in any city on earth.

STEVE MCQUEEN

There is no solitude in the world like that of the big
city.

KATHLEEN NORRIS

# Conversation

That is the happiest conversation where there is no competition, no vanity but a calm quiet interchange of sentiments.
SAMUEL JOHNSON
in Boswell, *Life of Johnson*, 1791

The wise man thinks once before he speaks twice.
ROBERT BENCHLEY

Civilized people can talk about anything.
CLIVE BELL
*Civilization*, 1928

There is nothing so good to the heart as well argued conversation, when you know that your companion will answer to your thought as the anvil meets the hammer ...
RICHARD JEFFERIES
*Nature Diaries and Notebooks*, 1948

Disagreement may be the shortest cut between two minds.
KAHLIL GIBRAN
*Sand and Foam*, 1954

There is no such thing as a convincing argument, although every man thinks he has one.
EDGAR WATSON HOWE
*Country Town Sayings*, 1911

Certain it is that scandal is good brisk talk, whereas praise of one's neighbour is by no means lively hearing. An acquaintance grilled, scored, devilled, and served with mustard and cayenne pepper excites the appetite; whereas a slice of cold friend with currant jelly is but a sickly, unrelishing meat.
THACKERAY
"Roundabout Papers"

# Conversation

We do not talk – we bludgeon one another with facts and theories gleaned from cursory readings of newspapers, magazines and digests.

HENRY MILLER
*The Air-Conditioned Nightmare*, 1945

He that guardeth his mouth keepeth his life:/But he that openeth wide his lips shall have destruction.

Proverbs, 13:3

It is not necessary to understand things in order to argue about them.

BEAUMARCHAIS

Most people are other people. Their thoughts are someone else's opinions, their life a mimicry, their passions a quotation.

OSCAR WILDE
*De Profundis*, 1905

To attack a man for talking nonsense is like finding your mortal enemy drowning in a swamp and jumping in after him with a knife.

KARL POPPER

Arguments are to be avoided; they are always vulgar and often convincing.

OSCAR WILDE
*The Importance of Being Earnest*, 1895

After all, the only proper intoxication is conversation.

OSCAR WILDE

# The Country

Untroubling and untroubled where I lie / The grass below, above, the vaulted sky.
JOHN CLARE
"I Am", 1865


Spring brought a flush of green wheat and there were violets under the hedges and pussy willows out beside the brook ... but only for a few weeks in later summer had the landscape any real beauty. Then the ripened cornfields rippled up to the doorsteps of the cottages and the hamlet became an island in a sea of dark gold.
FLORA THOMPSON
*Lark Rise to Candelford*, 1939


Good God! how sweet are all things here! / How beautiful the Fields appear! / How cleanly do we feed and lie! / Lord what good hours do we keep! / How quietly we sleep! / What peace! What unanimity!
CHARLES COTTON
"The Retirement"


All the sun long it was running, it was lovely, the hay / Fields high as the horse, the tunes from the chimneys, it was air, / And playing, lovely and watery / And fire green as grass.
DYLAN THOMAS
"Fern Hill"


Then, very early one morning, the men would come out of their houses, pulling on coats and lighting pipes as they hurried and calling to each other with skyward glances; "Think weather's a-gooin' to hold?" For three weeks or more during harvest the hamlet was astir before dawn and the homely odours of bacon frying, wood fires and tobacco smoke overpowered the pure, damp, earthy scent of the fields.
FLORA THOMPSON
*Lark Rise to Candelford*, 1939

# The Country

A man's soul may be buried and perish under a
dungheap or in a furrow of the field, just as under
a pile of money.

NATHANIEL HAWTHORNE
*Journals*, 1841

Lovers of the town have been content, for the most
part, to say they loved it. They do not brag about
its uplifting qualities. They have none of the
infernal smugness which makes the lover of the
country insupportable.

AGNES REPPLIER
*Times and Tendencies*, 1931

Anybody can be good in the country.

OSCAR WILDE
*Picture of Dorian Gray*, 1891

I have always felt a faint scepticism, a mild horror,
about the country. One goes for quiet; and a gang
of rooks is at work murderously tearing at the
furrows.

G. M. STONIER ("Fanfarlo")
*Shaving through the Blitz*

The lowest and vilest alleys of London do not
present a more dreadful record of sin than does the
smiling and beautiful countryside.

CONAN DOYLE
*The Adventures of Sherlock Holmes*, 1891

The wisest men, in the bulk, are the men who have
tilled the earth . . .
HILAIRE BELLOC
*The Silence of the Sea*, 1941


The sound of water escaping from mill-dams, etc,
willows, old rotten planks, shiny posts, and
brickwork, I love such things . . . those scenes
made me a painter and I am grateful.
JOHN CONSTABLE
in Leslie, *Life of John Constable*, 1843

To watch the progress of the crops is by no means
unentertaining to any rational creature.
WILLIAM COBBETT
*The English Gardener*, 1829


What would the world be, once bereft / Of wet and
wildness? Let them be left, / O let them be left,
wildness and wet; / Long live the weeds and the
wilderness yet.
GERARD MANLEY HOPKINS
"Inversnaid", 1881

Grant me, indulgent Heaven! a rural seat / Rather
contemptible than great.
NAHUM TATE
in Raymond Williams, *The Country and the City*,
1973

I live in the country. I have no other house. I am
impressed with certain things about farmers. One
of them is their destructiveness. One of them is
their total lack of the appreciation of the beautiful.

DR KARL HENNINGER<br>
A Psychiatrist's World

I have no relish for the country; it is a kind of
healthy grave.

SYDNEY SMITH, 1838

Rural life is a mystery until one realizes that nearly
all of it, everywhere in the world, is spent in
preparing for and recovering from short but
punishing bouts of the tedium inseparable from the
tasks of the land, or rather their failure to give the
least sense of achievement, as it might be a lifetime
spent washing up out of doors. I have never
understood why anybody agreed to go on being a
rustic after about 1400.

KINGSLEY AMIS<br>
The Green Man

.. the difference between town and country is
mostly the view.

NAN FAIRBROTHER<br>
New Lives, New Landscapes, 1970

We must therefore use some illusion to render a
Pastoral delightful; and this consists in exposing
the best side only of a shepherd's life, and in
concealing its miseries.

POPE

# Courage & Cowardice

The most mortifying infirmity in human nature, to feel in ourselves, or to contemplate in another, is, perhaps, cowardice.
CHARLES LAMB
*Last Essays of Elia,* 1833

If you can keep your head when all about you / are losing theirs . . .
KIPLING
"If"

Courage is grace under pressure.
ERNEST HEMINGWAY

Until the day of his death, no man can be sure of his courage.
JEAN ANOUILH
*Becket,* 1959

Courage is a kind of salvation.
PLATO
*The Republic,* 4th century B.C.

Life without the courage for death is slavery.
SENECA
*Letters to Lucilius,* 1st century A.D.

A high heart ought to bear calamities and not flee them, since in bearing them appears the grandeur of the mind and in fleeing them the cowardice of the heart.
PIETRO ARETINO, 1525

Come on you sons of bitches! Do you want to live for ever?
SGT DAN DALY, US Marines,
at the battle of Belleau Wood, June 1918

# Courage & Cowardice

The human race is a race of cowards: and I am not only marching in that procession but carrying a banner.

MARK TWAIN

If you can keep your head when all about you are losing theirs, it's just possible you haven't grasped the situation.

JEAN KERR<br>*Please Don't Eat the Daisies*, 1957

Love of fame, fear of disgrace, schemes for advancement, desire to make life comfortable and pleasant, and the urge to humiliate others are often at the root of the valour men hold in such high esteem.

LA ROCHEFOUCAULD<br>*Maxims*, 1665

A great part of courage is the courage of having done the thing before.

EMERSON<br>*The Conduct of Life*, 1860

Valour lies just half way between rashness and cowheartedness.

CERVANTES<br>*Don Quixote*, 1605–15

Sometimes even to live is an act of courage.

SENECA<br>*Letters to Lucilius*, 1st century A.D.

It is an easy thing for one whose foot / is on the outside of calamity / to give advice and to rebuke the sufferer.

AESCHYLUS<br>*Prometheus Bound*, c. 478 B.C.

Those that fly may fight again, / Which we can never do that's slain. / Hence timely running's no mean part / Of conduct, in the martial art.

SAMUEL BUTLER<br>*Hudibras*, 1663

# Crime & Punishment

Let us call it by the name which, for lack of any other nobility, will at least give the nobility of truth, and let us recognize it for what it essentially is: a revenge.
ALBERT CAMUS

Collective crimes incriminate no one.
NAPOLEON BONAPARTE
*Maxims*, 1804–15

The chief problem ... is not the punishment of criminals, but the preventing of the young from being trained to crime.
W. E. B. DU BOIS
*The Souls of Black Folk*, 1903

He that smiteth a man, so that he die, shall surely be put to death.
Exodus 21:12–13

Commit a crime, and the earth is made of glass. There is no such thing as concealment.
EMERSON
*Essays: First Series*, 1841

But if any mischief follow, then thou shalt give life for life, eye for eye, tooth for tooth, hand for hand, foot for foot, burning for burning, wound for wound, stripe for stripe.
Exodus 21:23–5

He who makes his law a curse, / By his own law shall surely die.
WILLIAM BLAKE
*Jerusalem*, 1804–20

He that spareth his rod hateth his son: But he that loveth him chasteneth him betimes.
Proverbs 13:24

When we neither punish nor reproach evildoers
... we are ripping the foundations of justice from
beneath new generations.

ALEXANDER SOLZHENITSYN

The number of malefactors authorizes not the
crime.

THOMAS FULLER<br>
Gnomologia, 1732

Juvenile delinquency serves many purposes,
including that of providing sadistic adults with
fantasies suited to their special tastes.

EDGAR Z. FRIEDENBERG<br>
The Vanishing Adolescent, 1959

Examination of the number of murders before and
after the abolition of the death penalty does not
support the theory that capital punishment has a
unique deterrent effect.

Capital Punishment, UN report, 1968

Every prison that men build / Is built with bricks of
shame, / And bound with bars lest Christ should
see / How men their brothers maim.

OSCAR WILDE<br>
The Ballad of Reading Gaol, 1898

The first of all laws is to respect the laws: the
severity of penalties is only a vain resource,
invented by little minds in order to substitute
terror for that respect which they have no means
of obtaining.

ROUSSEAU<br>
A Discourse on Political Economy, 1758

It is not the whip that makes men, but the lure of
things that are worthy to be loved.

WOODROW WILSON, 1906

I have never observed other effects of whipping
than to render boys more cowardly or more
wilfully obstinate.

MONTAIGNE

Beat your child once a day. If you don't know why,
he does.
Chinese proverb

You cannot do wrong without suffering wrong.
EMERSON
*Essays: First Series*, 1841

Fear succeeds crime – it is its punishment.
VOLTAIRE
*Sémiramis*, 1748

# Death

Death is a thing of grandeur. It brings instantly
into being a whole new network of relations
between you and the ideas, the desires, the habits
of the man now dead.
ANTOINE DE ST-EXUPÉRY
*Flight to Arras*, 1942

One should die proudly when it is no longer
possible to live proudly.
NIETZSCHE
*Twilight of the Idols*, 1889

I am sick of this way of life. The weariness and
sadness of old age make it intolerable. I have
walked with death in hand, and death's own hand
is warmer than my own. I don't wish to live any
longer.
W. SOMERSET MAUGHAM, on his ninetieth birthday

I'm all for bringing back the birch, but only
between consenting adults.

GORE VIDAL

All punishment is mischief. All punishment in itself
is evil.

JEREMY BENTHAM<br>
*Introduction to Principles of Morals and Legislation,*<br>
1789

Successful and fortunate crime is called virtue.

SENECA, 1st century A.D.

# Death

The last act is tragic, however happy all the rest of
the play is; at the last a little earth is thrown upon
our head, and that is the end for ever.

PASCAL<br>
*Pensées,* 1670

I'm not frightened of death. I just don't want to be
there when it happens.

WOODY ALLEN

It is a brave act of valour to contemn death; but
where life is more terrible than death, it is then the
truest valour to dare to live.

SIR THOMAS BROWNE<br>
*Religio Medici,* 1642

Our last garment is made without pockets.
Italian proverb


Death, the most dreaded of evils, is therefore of no
concern to us; for while we exist death is not
present, and when death is present we no longer
exist.
EPICURUS, 3rd century B.C.

Death is the supreme festival on the road to
freedom.
DIETRICH BONHOEFFER
*Letters and Papers from Prison*, 1953

To die is to go into the Collective Unconscious, to
lose oneself in order to be transformed into form,
into pure form.
HERMANN HESSE

I have asked for death. Begged for it. Prayed for it.
Then the worst thing can't be death.
ARCHIBALD MACLEISH
*JB*, 1958

Death is the supple suitor / That wins at last – / It
is a stealthy wooing / Conducted first / By pallid
innuendoes / And dim approach / But brave at last
with bugles.
EMILY DICKINSON
Untitled poem, *c.* 1878

The perpetual work of your life is but to lay the
foundation of death.
MONTAIGNE
*Essays*, 1580–88


Neither the sun nor death can be looked at
steadily.
LA ROCHEFOUCAULD
*Maxims*, 1665

If you can't take it with you, don't go!
                                    HEATHCOTE WILLIAMS
                                    *The Immortalist*, 1978

It hath oft been said, that it is not death, but dying,
which is terrible.

                                    HENRY FIELDING
                                    *Amelia*, 1751


But not all the preaching since Adam / Has made
Death other than Death.

                                    JAMES RUSSELL LOWELL
                                    "After the Burial", 1868

Death is the next step after the pension – it's
perpetual retirement without pay.

                                    JEAN GIRAUDOUX
                                    *The Enchanted*, 1933

Do not seek death. Death will find you.

                                    DAG HAMMERSKJÖLD
                                    *Markings*, 1964


Death does not blow a trumpet.

                                    Danish proverb




A belief in hell and the knowledge that every
ambition is doomed to frustration at the hands of
the skeleton have never prevented the majority of
human beings from behaving as though death
were no more than an unfounded rumour . . .

                                    ALDOUS HUXLEY
                                    *Themes and Variations*, 1950

He hath lived ill that knows not how to die well.

                                    THOMAS FULLER
                                    *Gnomologia*, 1732

Men fear death, as children fear to go in the dark;
and as that natural fear in children is increased
with tales, so is the other.
FRANCIS BACON
*Essays*, 1625

Our fear of death is like our fear that summer will
be short, but when we have had our swing of
pleasure, our fill of fruit, and our swelter of heat,
we say we have had our day.
EMERSON
*Journals*, 1855

There was a time when we were not: this gives us
no concern – why then should it trouble us that a
time will come when we shall cease to be?
WILLIAM HAZLITT
*Table Talk*, 1821–2

It's a funny old world – a man's lucky if he can get
out of it alive.
W. C. FIELDS
*You're Telling Me*, 1934

Death is the only pure, beautiful conclusion of a
great passion.
D. H. LAWRENCE
*Fantasia of the Unconscious*, 1923

Death holds no horrors. It is simply the ultimate
horror of life.

JEAN GIRAUDOUX
*The Enchanted*, 1933

Death always comes too early or too late.

English proverb

We dread life's termination as the close, not of
enjoyment, but of hope.

WILLIAM HAZLITT
*The Round Table*, 1817

On the plus side, death is one of the few things that
can be done as easily lying down.

WOODY ALLEN
*Getting Even*, 1972

We're all paid off in the end, and the fools first.

TALLULAH BANKHEAD

# Defence

Our sword keeps another in the sheath.
GEORGE HERBERT
*Jacula Prudentum,* 1651

It is an unfortunate fact that we can secure peace
only by preparing for war.
JOHN F. KENNEDY, 1960

At each epoch of history the world was in a
hopeless state, and at each epoch of history the
world muddled through; at each epoch, the world
was lost, and at each epoch it was saved.
JACQUES MARITAIN
*Reflections on America,* 1958

The discovery of the nuclear chain reaction need
not bring about the destruction of mankind any
more than did the discovery of matches.
ALBERT EINSTEIN, 1952

Neither a man nor a crowd nor a nation can be
trusted to act humanely or to think sanely under
the influence of a great fear.
BERTRAND RUSSELL
*Unpopular Essays,* 1950

The way to win an atomic war is to make certain it
never starts.
GENERAL OMAR BRADLEY, 1952

No absolute is going to make the lion lie down
with the lamb: unless the lamb is inside.
D. H. LAWRENCE

We will not act prematurely or unnecessarily risk
the costs of world-wide nuclear war in which even
the fruits of victory would be ashes in our mouth.
But neither will we shrink from that risk at any
time it must be faced.
JOHN F. KENNEDY, 1962

No country without an atom bomb could properly
consider itself independent.
CHARLES DE GAULLE, 1968

Whatever needs to be maintained by force is doomed.

HENRY MILLER
*The Wisdom of the Heart*, 1941

The basic problems facing the world today are not susceptible to a military solution.

JOHN F. KENNEDY

In the event of a nuclear war there will be no chances, there will be no survivors – all will be obliterated.

LORD LOUIS MOUNTBATTEN

The release of atom power has changed everything but our way of thinking and thus we are being driven unarmed towards a catastrophe. . . .

ALBERT EINSTEIN, 1946

To fear the worst oft cures the worse.

SHAKESPEARE
*Troilus and Cressida*, 1601–2

No nation ever had an army large enough to guarantee it against attack in time of peace or insure it victory in time of war.

CALVIN COOLIDGE, 1925

Our distrust justifies the deceit of others.

LA ROCHEFOUCAULD
*Maxims*, 1665

After the great destruction / Everyone will prove that he was innocent.

GÜNTER EICH
"Think of This", 1955

Suspicion on one side breeds suspicion on the other, and new weapons beget counterweapons.

JOHN F. KENNEDY, 1963

We are advocates of the abolition of war, we do not
want war; but war can only be abolished through
war . . .
MAO TSE-TUNG
*Quotations from Chairman Mao Tse-Tung*, 1966

The atomic bomb is another powerful weapon in
the arsenal of righteousness.
HARRY S. TRUMAN, 1945

Against naked force the only possible defence is
naked force. The aggressor makes the rules for
such a war; the defenders have no alternative but
matching destruction with more destruction,
slaughter with greater slaughter.
FRANKLIN D. ROOSEVELT, 1941

Shall I tell you what the real evil is? To cringe to
the things that are called evils, to surrender to
them our freedom in defiance of which we ought to
face any suffering.
SENECA
*Letters to Lucilius*, 1st century A.D.

The atom bomb is a paper tiger . . . Terrible to look
at but not so strong as it seems.
MAO TSE-TUNG

Since barbarism has its pleasures it naturally has
its apologists.

GEORGE SANTAYANA
*The Life of Reason: Reason in Society*, 1905–6

When evil acts in the world it always manages to
find instruments who believe that what they do is
not evil but honorable.

MAX LERNER
*The Unfinished Country*, 1959

The man who does evil to another does evil to
himself, / and the evil counsel is most evil for him
who counsels it.

HESIOD
*Works and Days*, 8th century B.C.

There are defeats more triumphant than victories.

MONTAIGNE
*Essays*, 1580–88

Cogito ergo boom.

SUSAN SONTAG
*Styles of Radical Will*, 1969

# Democracy

Democracy is the form of government in which the free are rulers.
ARISTOTLE
*Politics*, 4th century B.C.

Those self-important fathers of their country /
Think they're above the people. Why they're nothing! / The citizen is infinitely wiser.
EURIPIDES
*Andromache, c.* 426 B.C.

When the people rule, they must be rendered happy, or they will overturn the state.
DE TOCQUEVILLE
*Democracy in America,* 1835–9

Man's capacity for evil makes democracy necessary and man's capacity for good makes democracy possible.
REINHOLD NIEBUHR, 1977

If liberty and equality, as is thought by some, are chiefly to be found in democracy, they will be best attained when all persons alike share in the government to the utmost.
ARISTOTLE
*Politics*, 4th century B.C.

Democracy is the superior form of government, because it is based on a respect for man as a reasonable being.
JOHN F. KENNEDY
*Why England Slept,* 1940

All great movements are popular movements, volcanic eruptions of human passions. . . .
ADOLF HITLER
*Mein Kampf,* 1933

Democracy does not mean the coercion of all into a deadly, and finally wicked, mediocrity. But the best liberty for all to aspire to the best that is in him, or that ever has been.
JAMES BALDWIN, 1971

Democracy is a form of religion. It is the worship of jackals by jackasses.

H. L. MENCKEN

The blind lead the blind. It's the democratic way.

HENRY MILLER<br>
The Air-Conditioned Nightmare, 1945

Democracy is the theory that the common people know what they want, and deserve to get it good and hard.

H. L. MENCKEN<br>
A Book of Burlesques, 1920

In an autocracy, one person has his way; in an aristocracy a few people have their way; in a democracy no one has his way.

CELIA GREEN<br>
The Decline and Fall of Science

Let the people think they govern and they will be governed.

WILLIAM PENN<br>
Some Fruits of Solitude, 1693

No amount of charters, direct primaries, or short ballots will make a democracy out of an illiterate people.

WALTER LIPPMANN<br>
A Preface to Politics, 1914

One fifth of the people are against everything all the time.

ROBERT KENNEDY, 1964

Democracy means government by the uneducated, while aristocracy means government by the badly educated.

G. K. CHESTERTON, 1931

# Drinking

Man being reasonable, must get drunk; / The best of life is but intoxication.
BYRON
*Don Juan*, 1819–24

Any opiate is absolutely contra-indicated for a creative person, because it makes you less aware of what's happening around and inside you. . . . The writer is supposed to be more aware.
WILLIAM BURROUGHS, 1969

Long quaffing maketh a short life.
JOHN LYLY
*Euphues: The Anatomy of Wit*, 1579

O God, that men should put an enemy in their mouths to steal away their brains! that we should with joy, pleasance, revel, and applause transform ourselves into beasts.
SHAKESPEARE
*Othello*, 1604–5

Lechery, sir, it provokes, and unprovokes; it provokes the desire, but it takes away the performance.
SHAKESPEARE
*Macbeth*, 1605–6

We lived for days on nothing but food and water.
W. C. FIELDS

I'm an alcoholic, a genuine alcoholic. Not just a fake phoney alcoholic, I'm a real alcoholic.
TRUMAN CAPOTE, 1977

One reason I don't drink is that I want to know when I'm having a good time.
NANCY ASTOR

# Drinking

First you take a drink, then the drink takes a drink,
then the drink takes you.

F. SCOTT FITZGERALD
"The Crack-Up", 1936

No poems can please for long or live that are
written by water-drinkers.

HORACE
*Epistles, c.* 15 B.C.

There are more old drunkards than old doctors.
French proverb

Malt does more than Milton can, / To justify God's
ways to man.

A. E. HOUSMAN
*A Shropshire Lad*, 1896

. . . he that drinketh well, sleepeth well; he that
sleepeth well sinneth not; he that sinneth not
goeth straight through Purgatory to Paradise.

WILLIAM LITHGOW
*Rare Adventures*, 1614

Water taken in moderation cannot hurt anybody.

MARK TWAIN
*Notebook*, 1935

An alcoholic is someone you don't like who drinks
as much as you do.

DYLAN THOMAS

I don't drink. I don't like it. It makes me feel good.

OSCAR LEVANT, 1950

No man ever invented anything so bad as
drunkenness – or so good as drink.
G. K. CHESTERTON
*All Things Considered*, 1908


No government could survive without
champagne. Champagne in the throat of our
diplomatic people is like oil in the wheels of an
engine.
JOSEPH DARGENT, 1955

One more drink and I would be under the host.
DOROTHY PARKER
qu. John Keats, *You Might As Well Live*, 1971


# Duty

The last pleasure in life is the sense of discharging
our duty
WILLIAM HAZLITT
*Characteristics*, 1823


Without duty, life is soft and boneless; it cannot
hold itself together.
JOSEPH JOUBERT
*Pensées*, 1842

If a sense of duty tortures a man, it also enables
him to achieve prodigies.
H. L. MENCKEN
*Prejudices, First Series*, 1919

To an honest man, it is an honour to have
remembered his duty.
PLAUTUS
*The Three-Penny Day*, c. 194 B.C.

What does drunkenness not accomplish? It
unlocks secrets, confirms our hopes, urges the
indolent into battle, lifts the burden from anxious
minds, teaches new arts.

HORACE
*Epistles, c.* 15 B.C.

I hate champagne more than anything in the
world next to Seven-Up.

ELAINE DUNDY
*The Dud Avocado,* 1958

You're not drunk if you can lie on the floor
without holding on.

DEAN MARTIN

# Duty

In practice it is seldom very hard to do one's duty
when one knows what it is, but it is sometimes
exceedingly difficult to find this out.

SAMUEL BUTLER
*Note-Books,* 1912

Duty largely consists of pretending that the trivial
is critical.

JOHN FOWLES
*The Magus,* 1965

Duty is what one expects from others, it is not
what one does oneself.

OSCAR WILDE
*A Woman of No Importance,* 1893

When a stupid man is doing something he is
ashamed of, he always declares that it is his duty.

GEORGE BERNARD SHAW
*Caesar and Cleopatra,* 1906

A man is ethical only when life, as such, is sacred
to him, that of plants and animals as well as that of
his fellow man . . .
ALBERT SCHWEITZER

No man on earth is truly free / All are slaves of
money or necessity. / Public opinion or fear of
prosecution / forces each one, against his
conscience, to conform.
EURIPIDES
*Hecuba*, 425 B.C.

# Education

Only the educated are free.
EPICTETUS
*Discourses*, 2nd century A.D.

Education then, beyond all other devices of human
origin, is a great equalizer of the conditions of men,
– the balance wheel of the social machinery.
HORACE MANN, 1848

Education is not a *product*: mark, diploma, job,
money – in that order; it is a process, a never-
ending one.
BEL KAUFMAN, 1967

Define, define, well-educated infant.
SHAKESPEARE
*Love's Labour's Lost*, 1594–5

It is the duty of the free man to live for his own
sake, and not for others . . .

NIETZSCHE

Man exists for his own sake and not to add a
laborer to the State.

EMERSON<br>
Journals, 1839

# Education

School is necessary to produce the habits and
expectations of the managed consumer society.

IVAN ILLICH

Education makes a greater difference between man
and man than nature has between man and brute.

JOHN ADAMS, 1776

One by one the solid scholars / Get the degrees, the
jobs, the dollars.

W. D. SNODGRASS<br>
"April Inventory", 1959

Every definition is dangerous.

ERASMUS<br>
Adagio, 1500

Education is the leading human souls to what is best . . . the training which makes men happiest in themselves also makes them most serviceable to others.
RUSKIN
*The Stones of Venice*, 1851–3


Example is the best precept.
AESOP
*Fables*, 6th century B.C.


Education is an ornament in prosperity and a refuge in adversity.
ARISTOTLE, 4th century B.C.


Experience is the only teacher, and we get his lessons indifferently in any school.
EMERSON
*Journals*, 1845


Knowledge, in truth, is the great sun in the firmament.
DANIEL WEBSTER, 1825


All intellectuals complain about their schooldays. This is ridiculous.
LORD CLARK, 1974


Knowledge is power.
FRANCIS BACON
*Meditationes Sacrae*, 1597


To be master of any branch of knowledge, you must master those which lie next to it; and thus to know anything you must know all.
OLIVER WENDELL HOLMES, 1886

My degree was a kind of inoculation. I got just
enough of it to make me immune for the rest of my
life.

ALAN BENNETT
*Getting On*, 1974

No man was ever great by imitation.

SAMUEL JOHNSON
*Rasselas*, 1759

Soap and education are not as sudden as a
massacre, but they are more deadly in the long run.

MARK TWAIN
*Sketches New and Old*, 1900

Experience is the name everyone gives to their
mistakes.

OSCAR WILDE
*Lady Windermere's Fan*, 1892

I have learned throughout my life as a composer
chiefly through my mistakes and pursuits of false
assumptions, not by my exposure to founts of
wisdom and knowledge.

IGOR STRAVINSKY
*Themes and Episodes*, 1966

No one who had any sense has ever liked school.

LORD BOOTHBY, 1973

Knowledge is power. Unfortunate dupes of this
saying will keep on reading, ambitiously, till they
have stunned their native initiative, and made
their thoughts weak.

CLARENCE DAY
*This Simian World*, 1920

I am still of the opinion that only two topics can be
of the least interest to a serious and studious mind
– sex and the dead.

W. B. YEATS, 1927

Since we cannot be universal and know all that is
to be known of everything, we ought to know a
little about everything.
PASCAL
*Pensées*, 1670

... the race which does not value trained
intelligence is doomed.
ALFRED NORTH WHITEHEAD
*The Aims of Education*, 1932

All knowledge is of itself of some value. There is
nothing so minute or inconsiderable, that I would
not rather know it than not.
SAMUEL JOHNSON
in Boswell, *Life of Johnson*, 1775

Teachers who educate children deserve more
honour than parents ...
ARISTOTLE, 4th century B.C.


Delightful task! to rear the tender thought / To
teach the young idea how to shoot.
JAMES THOMSON
"Spring", 1726–30

Rather know nothing than half-know much.

NIETZSCHE<br>
Thus Spake Zarathustra, 1883–92

If I had learned education I would not have had
time to learn anything else.

CORNELIUS VANDERBILT

Knowledge is not an abstract homogeneous good,
of which there cannot be enough. Beyond the last
flutter of actual or possible significance, pedantry
begins.

JACQUES BARZUN

I dreamed last night I was teaching again – that's
the only bad dream that ever afflicts my sturdy
conscience.

D. H. LAWRENCE<br>
Selected Letters, 1950

Is education of the young the whole of life? I hate
the young – I'm worn out with them. They absorb
you and suck you dry and are vampires and selfish
brutes at best. Give me some good old rum-soaked
club men – who can't be improved . . . .

JOHN JAY CHAPMAN

# Fame

Fame – anyone who says he doesn't like it is crazy.
BENNETT CERF, 1964

Nothing arouses ambition as much in the heart as
the trumpet-clang of another's fame.
BALTASAR GRACIÁN
*The Art of Worldly Wisdom*, 1647

We're more popular than Jesus Christ now.
JOHN LENNON

All men desire fame. I have never known a single
exception to that rule, and I doubt if anyone else
has.
HILAIRE BELLOC
*The Silence of the Sea*, 1941

The day will come when everyone will be famous
for fifteen minutes.
ANDY WARHOL

Passion for fame: a passion which is the instinct of
all great souls.
EDMUND BURKE

Let fame, that all hunt after in their lives, / Live
register'd upon our brazen tombs, / And then
grace us in the disgrace of death.
SHAKESPEARE
*Love's Labour's Lost*, 1598

Famous men have the whole earth as their
memorial.
PERICLES
funeral oration, 430 B.C.

# Fame

If I'm such a legend, then why am I so lonely? ...
let me tell you, legends are all very well if you've
got somebody around who loves you ...

JUDY GARLAND

It is sobering to consider that when Mozart was my
age he had already been dead for a year.

TOM LEHRER

There is not a more unhappy being than a
superannuated idol.

JOSEPH ADDISON<br>The Spectator, 1711–12

Nothing is so common-place as to wish to be
remarkable.

OLIVER WENDELL HOLMES<br>The Autocrat of the Breakfast Table, 1857

In short, whoever you may be, / To this conclusion
you'll agree, / When everyone is somebodee, /
Then no one is anybody!

W. S. GILBERT<br>The Gondoliers, 1889

We all want to be famous people and the moment
we want to *be* something we are no longer free.

KRISHNAMURTI

Fame is a food that dead men eat, – / I have no
stomach for such meat.

AUSTIN DOBSON

I would give all my fame for a pot of ale ...

SHAKESPEARE<br>Henry V, 1600

# The Family

The family is the association established by nature for the supply of man's everyday wants.
ARISTOTLE
*Politics*, 4th century B.C.

When brothers agree, no fortress is so strong as their common life.
ANTISTHENES
5th–4th centuries B.C.

Happy is said to be the family which can eat onions together. They are, for the time being, separate from the world, and have a harmony of aspiration.
CHARLES DUDLEY WARNER
*My Summer in a Garden*, 1871

There's no vocabulary / For love within a family, love that's lived in / But not looked at, love within the light of which / All else is seen, the love within which / All other love finds speech.
T. S. ELIOT
*The Elder Statesman*, 1958

Without a family, man, alone in the world, trembles with the cold.
ANDRÉ MAUROIS
*The Art of Living*, 1940

The family is the test of freedom; because the family is the only thing that the free man makes for himself and by himself.
G. K. CHESTERTON
*Fancies versus Fads*, 1923

An ounce of blood is worth more than a pound of friendship.
Spanish proverb

# The Family

He that both wife and children hath given
hostages to fortune; for they are impediments to
great enterprises, either of virtue or mischief.

> FRANCIS BACON
> *Essays*, 1625

Cruel is the strife of brothers.

> ARISTOTLE
> *Politics*, 4th century B.C.

Happy families are all alike; every unhappy family
is unhappy in its own way.

> LEO TOLSTOY
> *Anna Karenina*, 1873–6

The Family! Home of all social evils, a charitable
institution for indolent women, a prison workshop
for the slaving breadwinner, and a hell for
children.

> AUGUST STRINDBERG
> *The Son of a Servant*, 1886

When a man is clutched by his family, his deeper
social instincts and intuitions are all thwarted, he
becomes a negative thing.

> D. H. LAWRENCE
> *Assorted Articles*, 1930

A family is but too often a commonwealth of
malignants.

> POPE
> *Thoughts on Various Subjects*, 1717

A married man with a family will do anything for
money.

> TALLEYRAND

# Fashion

Fine words and an insinuating appearance are
seldom associated with true virtue.
CONFUCIUS
*Analects*, 6th century B.C.

The apparel oft proclaims the man.
SHAKESPEARE
*Hamlet*, 1600

. . . the Lord seeth not as man seeth; for man
looketh on the outward appearance, but the Lord
looketh on the heart.
1 Samuel 16:7

A cheap coat makes a cheap man.
THORSTEIN VEBLEN
*The Theory of the Leisure Class*, 1899

What is more important in life than our bodies or
in the world than what we look like?
GEORGE SANTAYANA
*Persons and Places*, 1944

If you are not in fashion, you are nobody.
LORD CHESTERFIELD, 1750

By the husk you may guess the nut.
THOMAS FULLER
*Gnomologia*, 1732

The perfect woman must be haughty, but not too
beautiful . . . she must be a slave to her clothes and
her jewels.
SALVADOR DALI

A woman is as young as her knee.
MARY QUANT

One had as good be out of the world as out of
fashion.
COLLEY CIBBER
*Love's Last Shift*, 1696

If you've got it, flaunt it.

*anon*

A man becomes the creature of his uniform.

NAPOLEON BONAPARTE
*Maxims, 1804–15*

It is only shallow people who do not judge by appearances. The true mystery of the world is the visible, not the invisible.

OSCAR WILDE
*The Picture of Dorian Gray, 1891*

Under a bad cloak there is often a good drinker.

CERVANTES
*Don Quixote, 1605–15*

... style, like sheer silk, too often hides eczema.

ALBERT CAMUS
*The Fall, 1958*

The fear of becoming a "has been" keeps some people from becoming anything.

ERIC HOFFER
*The Passionate State of Mind, 1954*

'Tis not the habit that makes the monk.

THOMAS FULLER
*Gnomologia, 1732*

Don't ever wear artistic jewellery; it wrecks a woman's reputation.

COLETTE
*Gigi*

Wearing her skirt half way up the thigh does not give a woman the advantage.

COCO CHANEL, 1967

Fashion is made to become unfashionable.

COCO CHANEL, 1957

A man with a good coat upon his back meets with
a better reception than he who has a bad one.
SAMUEL JOHNSON
in Boswell, *Life of Johnson*, 1791

Good taste is better than bad taste, but bad taste is
better than no taste.
ARNOLD BENNETT, 1930

Style is knowing who you are, what you want to
say, and not giving a damn.
GORE VIDAL, 1973

# Fate

We are ruled by chance but never have enough
patience to accept its despotism.
EDWARD DAHLBERG
*Reasons of the Heart*, 1965

Chance makes a plaything of man's life.
SENECA
*Letters to Lucilius*, 1st century A.D.

What the reason of the ant laboriously drags into a
heap, the wind of accident will collect in one
breath.
SCHILLER
*Fiesco*, 1783

Fine clothes are good only as they supply the want
of other means of procuring respect.
SAMUEL JOHNSON
in Boswell, *Life of Johnson*, 1791

Exuberance is better than taste.
GUSTAVE FLAUBERT
*Sentimental Education*, 1869

I don't believe in style. I want to be a machine.
ANDY WARHOL

## Fate

Shallow men believe in luck ... strong men believe
in cause and effect.
EMERSON
*The Conduct of Life*, 1860

Man is not the creature of circumstances.
Circumstances are the creatures of men.
DISRAELI
*Vivian Grey*, 1826

The people who get on in this world are the people
who get up and look for the circumstances they
want, and if they can't find them, make them.
GEORGE BERNARD SHAW
*Mrs Warren's Profession*, 1898

One of the many lessons that one learns in prison
is, that things are what they are and will be what
they will be.
OSCAR WILDE
*De Profundis*, 1905

I have always believed that all things depended
upon Fortune, and nothing upon ourselves.
BYRON

Anatomy is destiny.
SIGMUND FREUD

Failure or success seem to have been allotted to
men by their stars. But they retain the power of
wriggling, of fighting with their star or against it,
and in the whole universe the only really
interesting movement is this wriggle.
E. M. FORSTER
*Abinger Harvest*, 1936

We talk about fate as if it were something visited
upon us; we forget that we create our fate every
day we live.

HENRY MILLER


I was thinking of my patients, and how the worst
moment for them was when they discovered they
were masters of their own fate. It was not a matter
of bad or good luck. When they could no longer
blame fate, they were in despair.

ANAÏS NIN<br>
*The Journals*, vol. II, 1967

Intellect annuls fate. So far as a man thinks, he is
free.

EMERSON

The fault, dear Brutus, is not in our Stars, / But in
ourselves that we are underlings.

SHAKESPEARE<br>
*Julius Caesar*, 1599

... certainly we need rebellion. Unless woman is going to make trouble she had better not seek her emancipation.
REBECCA WEST


The extension of women's rights is the basic principle of all social progress.
CHARLES FOURIER
*Théorie des Quatre Mouvements*, 1808


Women's past is at least as rich as men's; that we do not know about it, that we encounter only silence when we seek it, is part of our oppression.
DALE SPENDER
*Women of Ideas*, 1982


All women are Lesbians, except those who don't know it yet.
JILL JOHNSTON
*Dialog on Women's Liberation*, 1971


My God, if women hadde written stories / As clerics hav with-inne hir oratories, / They wolde han written of men more wicked verse, / Than all the mark of Adam may redress.
CHAUCER
*Wife of Bath's Tale, c.* 1387


But if God had wanted us to think with our wombs, why did he give us a brain?
CLARE BOOTH LUCE


Whatever women do they must do twice as well as men to be thought half as good. Luckily, this is not difficult.
CHARLOTTE WHITTON


Women are equal because they are not different any more.
ERICH FROMM
*The Art of Loving*, 1956

Let the woman learn in silence with all
subjection. / But I suffer not a woman to teach, nor
to usurp authority over the man, but to be in
silence.

1 Timothy 2:11

A woman who thinks she is intelligent demands
equal rights with men. A woman who *is* intelligent
does not.

COLETTE

The happiest women, like the happiest nations,
have no history.

GEORGE ELIOT
*The Mill on the Floss,* 1860

Silly women laden with sins, led away with divers
lusts.

2 Timothy 3:6

The average girl would rather have beauty than
brains because she knows that the average man
can see much better than he can think.

*Ladies' Home Journal,* 1947

It is hard to fight an enemy who has outposts in
your head.

SALLY KEMPTON, 1970

A woman who strives to be like a man lacks
ambition.

graffito

Equality is a myth – women are better.

graffito

If a woman's husband gets on her nerves she
should fly at him. . . . She should lead him a dog's
life, and never swallow her bile . . . . Wives, don't
love husbands nor your children, nor anybody . . .
don't let him drive you out of your solitude, your
singleness within yourself.
D. H.LAWRENCE
*Fantasia of the Unconscious*, 1923


Life in this society being, at best, an utter bore and
no aspect of society being at all relevant to women,
there remains to civic-minded, responsible, thrill-
seeking females only to overthrow the
government, eliminate the money system, institute
complete automation and destroy the male sex.
VALERIE SOLANAS
*SCUM* [Society for Cutting Up Men] *Manifesto*, 1967


At the worst, a house unkept cannot be so
distressing as a life unlived.
ROSE MACAULAY


The point of Women's Liberation is not to stand at
the door of the male world, beating our fists, and
crying: "Let me in, damn you, let me in!" The
point is to walk away from that world and concen-
trate on creating a new woman, a woman who will
take no place in that world, a woman who will
make that world fall by refusing to populate it . . .
VIVIAN GORNICK
Introduction to *SCUM Manifesto*, 1967


Home is the girl's prison and the woman's
workhouse.
GEORGE BERNARD SHAW'

He that has lost a wife and sixpence has lost
sixpence.

Scottish proverb

You have to go back to the Children's Crusade in
1212 A.D. to find as unfortunate and fatuous an
attempt at manipulated hysteria as the Women's
Liberation Movement.

HELEN LAWRENSON, 1971

A woman should be as proud of her success in
making her house into a perfect little world as the
greatest statesman of his in organizing a nation's
affairs.

ANDRÉ MAUROIS<br>
The Art of Living, 1940

God made the woman for the man, / And for the
good and increase of the world.

TENNYSON<br>
"Edwin Morris", 1842

There is no spectacle on earth more appealing
than that of a beautiful woman in the act of
cooking dinner for someone she loves.

THOMAS WOLFE<br>
The Web and the Rock, 1939

Women have very little idea of how much men
hate them.
GERMAINE GREER
*The Female Eunuch,* 1970

A woman's work is never done by men.
graffito

It takes a brave man to face a brave woman, and
man's fear of woman's creative energy has never
found an expression more clear than ... "Kinder,
Kuche, Kirche," for women.
PEARL S. BUCK
*To My Daughters, With Love,* 1967

# Food

Serenely full, the epicure would say / Fate cannot
harm me, I have dined today.
SYDNEY SMITH

Cookery has become an art, a noble science; cooks
are gentlemen.
BURTON
*The Anatomy of Melancholy,* 1621

Beans, beans, the musical fruit / The more you eat
the more you toot. / The more you toot, the better
you feel. / So eat your beans with every meal.
THOMAS TANSSIK

*Pastasciutta,* however grateful to the palate, is an
absolute food; it is heavy, brutalising and gross; its
nutritive qualities are deceptive; it induces
scepticism, sloth and pessimism ... our
pastasciutta, like our rhetoric, suffices merely to fill
the mouth.
MARINETTI, 1930

Every man is wanted, and no man is wanted
much.

EMERSON<br>
Essays, Second Series, 1844

When female minds are embittered . . . their
malignity is generally exerted in a rigorous and
spiteful superintendence of domestic trifles.

SAMUEL JOHNSON<br>
The Rambler, 1750

They have a right to work wherever they want to –
as long as they have dinner ready when you get
home.

JOHN WAYNE

# Food

A glutton digs his own grave with his teeth.

English proverb

God sends meat and the Devil sends cooks.

English proverb

There is no dignity in the bean.

CHARLES DUDLEY WARNER<br>
My Summer in the Garden, 1871

The angels in Paradise eat nothing but vermicelli al
pomodoro.

DUKE OF BOVINO, in reply to Marinetti

Seeing's believing, but feeling's the truth.
THOMAS FULLER
*Gnomologia*, 1732

At a dinner party one should eat wisely but not too
well, and talk well, but not too wisely.
SOMERSET MAUGHAM
*A Writer's Notebook*, 1949

An oyster, that m irvel of delicacy, that
concentration of sapid excellence, that mouthful
before all other mouthfuls . . .
HENRY WARD BEECHER

You got very hungry when you did not eat enough
in Paris . . . I learned to understand Cézanne much
better and to see truly how he made landscapes
when I was hungry.
ERNEST HEMINGWAY
*A Moveable Feast*, 1960

Vegetarianism is harmless enough, though it is apt
to fill a man with wind and self-righteousness.
SIR ROBERT HUTCHINSON

Seeing is deceiving. It's eating that's believing.
JAMES THURBER
*Further Fables for Our Time*, 1956

Conversation is the enemy of good wine and food.
ALFRED HITCHCOCK, 1978

It's a wery remarkable circumstance, Sir, that
poverty and oysters always seem to go together. . . .
Bless me, if I don't think that ven a man's wery
poor he rushes out and eats oysters in reglar
desperation.
SAM WELLER
in Dickens, *Pickwick Papers*, 1836–7

I've known what it is to be hungry, but I always
went right to a restaurant.
RING LARDNER

And Mr Mick . . . at length declared vegetarianism
doomed ("shedding", as he called it finely, "the
green blood of the silent animals") and predicted
that men in a better age would live entirely on salt.
G. K. CHESTERTON
*The Napoleon of Notting Hill*, 1904

# Friendship

God gives us our relations, but thank God we can
choose our friends.
English proverb

Peace dies when the framework is ripped apart. . . .
When you know no longer where your friend is to
be found.
SAINT-EXUPÉRY
*Flight to Arras*, 1942

Friends are at their best in moments of defeat.
HENRY MILLER
*Sexus*, 1949

Count not him among your friends who will retail
your privacy to the world.
PUBILILIUS SYRUS
*Moral Sayings*, 1st century B.C.

When a friend is in trouble, don't annoy him by
asking if there is anything you can do. Think up
something appropriate and do it.
E. W. HOWE
*Country Town Sayings*, 1911

Old friends are the great blessing of one's later
years – half a word conveys one's meaning.
HORACE WALPOLE

It is more shameful to distrust one's friends than to
be deceived by them.
LA ROCHEFOUCAULD
*Maxims*, 1665

thou hast great allies / Thy friends are exultations
. . .
WILLIAM WORDSWORTH
"To Toussaint L'Ouverture", 1803

Friends are God's apology for relations.

HUGH KINGSMILL

To find a friend one must close one eye; to keep him – two.

NORMAN DOUGLAS

When you are down and out, something always turns up – and it is usually the noses of your friends.

ORSON WELLES, 1962

There is only one thing in the world worse than being talked about, and that is not being talked about.

OSCAR WILDE<br>*The Picture of Dorian Gray*, 1891

There's nothing in the world I wouldn't do for Hope, and there's nothing in the world he wouldn't do for me. . . . We spend our lives doing nothing for each other.

BING CROSBY, 1950

It is in the thirties that we want friends. In the forties we know they won't save us any more than love did.

F. SCOTT FITZGERALD<br>"The Crack-Up", 1936

When your friend holds you affectionately by both hands you are safe, for you can watch both his.

AMBROSE BIERCE

Whenever a friend succeeds, a little something in me dies.

GORE VIDAL, 1973

What was Paradise? but a garden, an orchard of trees and herbs, full of pleasure, and nothing there but delights.
WILLIAM LAWSON
*A New Orchard and Garden,* 1618

Oh how sweet and pleasant is the fruit of those trees which a man hath planted and ordered with his owne hand, to gather it, and freely to bestow it among kindred and friends.
RALPH AUSTEN, 1653

*Rosa filipes* "Kiftsgate". An extremely vigorous rose that has been known to spread to as much as 50ft across. Massive heads of small, sweetly scented, creamy-white flowers, followed by small oval hips. A wonderful rose for growing over bushes and into trees, or for covering unsightly buildings, wherever space allows.
*David Austen's Rose Catalogue*

Into your garden you can walk / And with each plant and flower talk / View all their glories, from each one / Raise some rare meditation.
JOHN REA
*Flora, Ceres and Pomona,* 1665

There are fairies at the bottom of our garden.
ROSE FYLEMAN
*Fairies and Chimneys,* 1918

If you would be happy for a week, take a wife; if you would be happy for a month, kill your pig: but if you would be happy all your life, plant a garden.
Chinese saying

Airborne filth settling on aphis honey-dew would
asphyxiate all those plants which survive the
sucking, biting, chewing, riddling activities of the
insects, if it were not for the fact that they are
generally pecked to death by sparrows, dug up,
trodden on, sat on or stolen, or simply annihilated
by a blast of animal urine or overwhelmed by a
cloaking turd, long before that.

> "Rose Blight" (GERMAINE GREER)
> *The Revolting Garden*, 1979

One queer thing about / spring gardens is / that so
many people / use them to / raise spinach in /
instead of food.

> DON MARQUIS
> *Archy's Life of Mehitabel*, 1934

*Rosa filipes* "Kiftsgate" is able to strangle full-
grown elms. The euphoric freak, about whom she
throws her hammerlock, will indeed die in
aromatic pain. If he struggles to break free of her
iron caress he may well flay himself to the bone.

> "Rose Blight" (GERMAINE GREER)
> *The Revolting Garden*, 1979

"Hurrah! blister my kidneys," exclaimed he in
delight, "it is a frost! – the dahlias are dead."

> R. S. SURTEES
> *Handley Cross*, 1843

Nothing grows in our garden, only washing / And
babies.

> DYLAN THOMAS
> *Under Milk Wood*

GR-R-R- there go, my heart's abhorrence! / Water
your damned flower-pots do! / If hate killed men,
Brother Lawrence, / God's blood, would not mine
kill you! / What? your myrtle-bush wants
trimming? / Oh, that rose has prior claims – /
Needs its leaden vase filled brimming? / Hell dry
you up with its flames!

> ROBERT BROWNING
> "Soliloquy of the Spanish Cloister", 1863

# Goodness

Few persons have courage enough to appear as good as they really are.
JULIUS CHARLES HARE & AUGUSTUS WILLIAM HARE
*Guesses at Truth*, 1827

The example of good men is visible philosophy.
English proverb

An honest man's word is as good as his bond.
CERVANTES
*Don Quixote*, 1605–15

Be ye kind one to another, even as God also in Christ forgave you.
Ephesians 4:32

Every good gift and every perfect boon is from above ...
James 1:17

No legacy is so rich as honesty.
SHAKESPEARE
*All's Well That Ends Well*, 1602–3

We believe that civilization has been built up ... by sacrifices in gratification of the primitive impulses.
SIGMUND FREUD
*Introductory Lectures*, 1917

If thine enemy be hungry, give him bread to eat;
And if he be thirsty, give him water to drink.
Proverbs 25:21

We come nearest to the great when we are great in humility.
RABINDRANATH TAGORE
*Stray Birds*, 1916

# Goodness

There is no man so good, who, were he to submit
all his thoughts and actions to the laws, would not
deserve hanging ten times in his life.

MONTAIGNE
*Essays*, 1580–88

Few things are harder to put up with than the
annoyance of good example.

MARK TWAIN
*Pudd'nhead Wilson*, 1894

A verbal agreement isn't worth the paper it's
written on.

LOUIS B. MAYER

Never Give a Sucker an Even Break

W. C. FIELDS, film title

Presents believe me, seduce both men and gods.

OVID
*The Art of Love*, A.D. 8

Honesty for the most part is less profitable than
dishonesty.

PLATO
*The Republic*, 4th century B.C.

If you resolve to give up smoking, drinking and
loving, you don't actually live longer; it just seems
longer.

CLEMENT FREUD (attrib.)

Whenever thy hand can ready it, tear out thy foe's
brain, for such an opportunity washes anger from
the mind.

SA'DI
*Gulistan*, 1258

Humility is not the renunciation of pride, but the
substitution of one pride for another.

ERIC HOFFER
*The Passionate State*, 1954

If thou have any good things believe better things
of others that thou may keep thy meekness.
THOMAS À KEMPIS
*The Imitation of Christ*, 1426

Men always love what is good . . .
ROUSSEAU
*The Social Contract*, 1762

Until man learns to accept his fellow man with all
his faults, as well as his virtues, there can be no
peace, no joy, no real understanding.
HENRY MILLER
*Ecce Homo*, 1967

We are healthy only to the extent that our ideas
are humane.
KURT VONNEGUT jr

Blessed are the meek: for they shall inherit the
earth.
Matthew 5:5

To think ill of mankind, and not wish ill to them, is
perhaps the highest wisdom and virtue.
WILLIAM HAZLITT
*Characteristics*, 1823

Dare to be true: nothing can need a lie.
GEORGE HERBERT
"The Temple"

*Meekness.* n. Uncommon patience in planning a
revenge that is worth while.

AMBROSE BIERCE<br>
The Devil's Dictionary, 1881–1911

All men naturally hate one another. They employ
lust as far as possible in the service of the public
weal. But this is only a pretence and a false image
of love, for at bottom it is only hate.

PASCAL<br>
Pensées, 1670

Patience has its limits. Take it too far and it's
cowardice.

GEORGE JACKSON, 1970

A humanitarian is always a hypocrite.

GEORGE ORWELL

Pity the meek, for they shall inherit the earth.

DON MARQUIS

Be on your guard against the good and the just!
They would fair crucify those who devise their
own virtue – they hate the lonesome ones.

NIETZSCHE<br>
Thus Spake Zarathustra, 1883–92

Without lies humanity would perish of despair and
boredom.

ANATOLE FRANCE<br>
The Bloom of Life, 1922

# Government

The divine science of government is social happiness, and the blessings of society depend entirely on the constitutions of government.
JOHN ADAMS
*Discourses on Davila*, 1789

... the happiness of the people is the sole end of the government.
JOHN ADAMS, 1774

I hate all bungling like sin, but most of all bungling in state affairs, which produces nothing but mischief to thousands and millions.
GOETHE
in Eckermann, *Conversations with Goethe*, 1847

Lawful and settled authority is very seldom resisted when it is well employed.
SAMUEL JOHNSON
*The Rambler*, 1750–52

You can't fool all of the people all the time.
ABRAHAM LINCOLN

Power tends to corrupt, and absolute power corrupts absolutely.
LORD ACTON

There is only one political career for which women are perfectly suited: diplomacy.
CLARE BOOTH LUCE

In order that people may be free, it is necessary that the governed be sages and those who govern gods.
NAPOLEON BONAPARTE

Government is a contrivance of human wisdom to provide for human wants. Men have a right that these wants should be provided for by this wisdom.
EDMUND BURKE

Man is about the same in the main, whether with despotism, or whether with freedom.

WALT WHITMAN
*Notes Left Over*, 1881

I would not give half-a-guinea to live under one form of government rather than another. It is of no moment to the happiness of the individual.

SAMUEL JOHNSON
in Boswell, *Life of Johnson*, 1791

Whenever you have efficient government you have a dictatorship.

HARRY S. TRUMAN

Authority is never without hate.

EURIPIDES
*Ion*, 5th century B.C.

You can fool too many of the people too much of the time.

JAMES THURBER
*The Thurber Carnival*, 1945

Power corrupts, but lack of power corrupts absolutely.

ADLAI STEVENSON

Diplomacy is the police in grand costume.

NAPOLEON BONAPARTE

The only good government . . . is a bad one in a hell of a fright.

JOYCE CARY
*The Horse's Mouth*, 1944

Despotism tempered by assassination.

LORD REITH, on the best form of government

# Happiness

The right to happiness is fundamental: / Men live so little time and die alone.
BERTOLT BRECHT
*The Threepenny Opera*, 1928

... I have the true feeling of myself only when I am unbearably unhappy.
FRANZ KAFKA
*The Diaries: 1914–23*

Good friends, good books and a sleepy conscience: this is the ideal life.
MARK TWAIN
*Notebook*, 1935

You are forgiven for your happiness and your success only if you generously consent to share them.
ALBERT CAMUS
*The Fall*, 1956

Resolve to be thyself: and know, that he / Who finds himself, loses his misery.
MATTHEW ARNOLD
"Self-Dependence", 1852

That man is happiest / Who lives from day to day and asks no more, / Garnering the simple goodness of a life.
EURIPIDES
*Hecuba*, 425 B.C.

Lying in bed would be an altogether perfect and supreme experience if only one had a coloured pencil long enough to draw on the ceiling.
G. K. CHESTERTON
*Tremendous Trifles*, 1909

Happiness is not the end of life: character is.

HENRY WARD BEECHER
*Life Thoughts*, 1858

... melancholy and remorse form the deep leaden keel which enables us to sail into the wind of reality; we run aground sooner than the flat-bottomed pleasure-lovers, but we venture out in weather that would sink them, and we choose our direction.

CYRIL CONNOLLY
*The Unquiet Grave*, 1944

Contentment is a warm sty for the eaters and sleepers.

EUGENE O'NEILL
*Marco Millions*, 1928

I have not a word to say against contented people so long as they keep quiet.... If you are foolish enough to be contented, don't show it, but grumble with the rest.

JEROME K. JEROME
*The Idle Thoughts of an Idle Fellow*, 1889

I have always disliked myself at any given moment; the total of such moments is my life.

CYRIL CONNOLLY
*Enemies of Promise*, 1938

Oh don't the days seem lank and long, / When all goes right and nothing goes wrong / And isn't your life extremely flat / With nothing whatever to grumble at!

W. S. GILBERT
*Princess Ida*, 1884

Happy men are grave. They carry their happiness cautiously, as they would a glass filled to the brim, which the slightest movement could cause to spill over or break.

BARBEY D'AUREVILLY
*Les Diaboliques*, 1874

Happiness depends upon ourselves.
ARISTOTLE
*Nicomachean Ethics*, 4th century B.C.


Jealousy and anger shorten life, and anxiety brings
on old age too soon.
Ecclesiasticus 30:24


The Possible's slow fuse is lit / By the Imagination.
EMILY DICKINSON
*Poems*, 1862


The practice of self-denial is good; it may be learnt.
More difficult than self-denial is enjoyment,
rejoicing in that which ought to delight us. This
perhaps may be partly learnt, but not without
severest discipline.
MARK RUTHERFORD


Happiness is the rational understanding of life and
the world.
SPINOZA

Hope is the great falsifier of truth.
BALTASAR GRACIÁN
*The Art of Worldly Wisdom*, 1647

Every man's happiness is built on the unhappiness
of others.

TURGENEV
*On the Eve*, 1860

Joy interrupted now and again by pain and
terminated ultimately by death seems the normal
course of life in Nature. Anxiety and distress,
interrupted occasionally by pleasure, is the normal
course of man's existence.

JOSEPH WOOD KRUTCH
*The Twelve Seasons*, 1949

Were it not for imagination, a man would be as
happy in the arms of a chambermaid as of a
duchess.

SAMUEL JOHNSON
in Boswell, *Life of Johnson*, 1791

The man who thoroughly enjoys what he reads or
does, or even what he says, or simply what he
dreams or imagines, profits to the full. The man
who *seeks* to profit, through one form of discipline
or another, deceives himself.

HENRY MILLER
*The Books in my Life*, 1952

Happiness? That's nothing more than health and a
poor memory.

ALBERT SCHWEITZER

Hope, deceitful as it is, serves at least to lead us to
the end of our lives by an agreeable route.

LA ROCHEFOUCAULD
*Maxims*, 1665

# History

History teaches us that men and nations behave
wisely once they have exhausted all other
alternatives.
ABBA EBAN, 1970

History is the essence of innumerable biographies.
THOMAS CARLYLE

Those who do not remember the past are
condemned to relive it.
GEORGE SANTAYANA
*The Life of Reason*, 1905

The past has revealed to me the structure of the
future.
TEILHARD DE CHARDIN
*Letters from a Traveller*, 1962

History provides neither compensation for
suffering nor penalties for wrong.
LORD ACTON, 1887

Old custom is hard to break and scarce any man
will be lead otherwise than seemeth good unto
himself.
THOMAS À KEMPIS
*The Imitation of Christ*, 1426

The golden age was never the present age.
Proverb

The talent of historians lies in their creating a true
ensemble out of facts which are but half true.
ERNEST RENAN
*La Vie de Jésus*, 1863

History repeats itself. That's one of the things
wrong with history.
CLARENCE DARROW

History is an endless repetition of the wrong way of living.

LAWRENCE DURRELL, 1978

Biographies are but the clothes and buttons of the man – the biography of the man himself cannot be written.

MARK TWAIN<br>
*Autobiography*, 1924

Peoples and governments have never learned anything from history, or acted on principles deduced from it.

HEGEL<br>
*Philosophy of History*, 1832

Life could not continue without throwing the past into the past, liberating the present from its burden.

PAUL TILLICH<br>
*The Eternal Now*, 1963

History is bunk.

HENRY FORD

How many things, both just and unjust, are sanctioned by custom!

TERENCE<br>
*The Self-Tormentor*, 163 B.C.

People think too historically. They are always living half in a cemetery.

ARISTIDE BRIAND

History is a set of lies agreed upon.

NAPOLEON BONAPARTE

"History repeats itself," and "History never repeats itself," are about equally true.

G. M. TREVELYAN

History is a record of human progress, a record of the struggle of the advancement of the human mind, of the human spirit, toward some known or unknown object.
NEHRU

History is a cyclic poem written by time upon the memories of man.
SHELLEY

History is philosophy teaching by examples.
HENRY ST JOHN, LORD BOLINGBROKE

## Justice & The Law

Justice is the right of the weakest.
JOSEPH JOUBERT
*Pensées*, 1842


Justice is truth in action.
JOSEPH JOUBERT
*Pensées*, 1842


We do not get good laws to restrain bad people. We get good people to restrain bad laws.
G. K. CHESTERTON
*All Things Considered*, 1908

An unjust law is itself a species of violence. Arrest for its breach is more so.
M. K. GANDHI
*Non-Violence in Peace and War*, 1948

Historians are like deaf people who go on
answering questions that no one has asked them.

TOLSTOY

History repeats itself; historians repeat each other.

PHILIP GUEDALLA

History is a nightmare from which we are trying to
wake.

JAMES JOYCE

# Justice & The Law

Everywhere there is one principle of justice, which
is the interest of the stronger.

PLATO<br>
The Republic, 4th century B.C.

The lawyer's truth is not Truth, but consistency or
a consistent expediency.

THOREAU<br>
Civil Disobedience, 1849

I don't want a lawyer to tell me what I cannot do; I
hire him to tell me how to do what I want to do.

J. PIERPOINT MORGAN

Anyone who takes it upon himself, on his own
authority, to break a bad law, thereby authorizes
everyone else to break the good ones.

DENIS DIDEROT, 1796

Justice has become a biological necessity in man.
DR JACOB BRONOWSKI


The judge should not be young; he should have
learned to know evil, not from his own soul, but
from late and long observation of the nature of evil
in others.
PLATO
*The Republic*, 4th century B.C.

All virtue is summed up in dealing justly.
ARISTOTLE
*Nicomachean Ethics*, 4th century B.C.

Let all the laws be clear, uniform and precise; to
interpret laws is almost always to corrupt them.
VOLTAIRE
*Philosophical Dictionary*, 1764

Our nation is founded on the principle that
observance of the law is the eternal safeguard of
liberty and defiance of the law is the surest road to
tyranny.
JOHN F. KENNEDY, 1962

Where law ends, tyranny begins.
WILLIAM PITT THE ELDER


The law is reason free from passion.
ARISTOTLE
*Ethics*, 4th century B.C.

There is scarcely anything more important in the
government of men than the exact – I will even say
the pedantic – observance of the regular forms by
which the guilt or innocence of accused persons is
determined.
SIR WINSTON CHURCHILL

The certitude of laws is an obscurity of judgment
backed only by authority.
GIAMBATTISTA VICO<br>
The New Science, 1725–44

Judges commonly are elderly men, and are more
likely to hate at sight any analysis to which they
are not accustomed, and which disturbs repose of
mind, than to fall in love with novelties.
OLIVER WENDELL HOLMES, 1899

There is no such thing as justice in the abstract; it
is merely a compact between men.
EPICURUS, 3rd century B.C.

A jury consists of twelve persons chosen to decide
who has the better lawyer.
ROBERT FROST

A man's respect for law and order exists in precise
relationship to the size of his paycheck.
ADAM CLAYTON POWELL<br>
Keep the Faith, Baby!, 1967

No law is quite appropriate for all.
LIVY<br>
Ab Urbe Condita, c. 29 B.C.

People say law but they mean wealth.
EMERSON<br>
Journals, 1839

We see neither justice nor injustice which does not
change its nature with change in climate. Three
degrees of latitude reverse all jurisprudence; a
meridian decides the truth.
BLAISE PASCAL<br>
Pensées, 1670

# Leadership

It is the characteristic excellence of the strong man
that he can bring momentous issues to the fore
and make a decision about them.
DIETRICH BONHOEFFER
*Letters and Papers from Prison*, 1953


Some are born great, some achieve greatness, and
some have greatness thrust upon 'em.
SHAKESPEARE
*Twelfth Night*, 1599–1600


There are men, who, by their sympathetic
attractions, carry nations with them, and lead the
activity of the human race.
EMERSON
*The Conduct of Life*, 1860


Government after all is a very simple thing.
WARREN G. HARDING


The ordinary man is involved in action, the hero
acts. An immense difference.
HENRY MILLER
*The Books in My life*, 1952


One can never be sure that when a man becomes
the President of the United States his sense of
power and of purpose and his own source of self
confidence will show him how to help himself
enhance his personal influence. . . . The Presidency
is no place for amateurs.
RICHARD NEUSTADT
*Presidential Power*, 1964


Let us begin by committing ourselves to the truth,
to see it like it is and to tell it like it is, to find the
truth, to speak the truth and live with the truth.
That's what we'll do.
RICHARD M. NIXON, 1968

Too much has been said of the heroes of history –
the strong men, the troublesome men; too little of
the amiable, the kindly, and the tolerant.

STEPHEN LEACOCK

Some are born great, some achieve greatness, and
some hire public relations officers.

DANIEL BOORSTIN
*The Image*, 1962

The real leader has no need to lead – he is content
to point the way.

HENRY MILLER
*The Wisdom of the Heart*, 1941

I can't make a damn thing out of this tax problem.
I listen to one side and they seem right – and then I
talk to the other side and they seem just as right,
and here I am where I started. God, what a job!

WARREN G. HARDING

The chief business of the nation, as a nation, is the
setting up of heroes, mainly bogus.

H. L. MENCKEN
*Prejudices, Third Series*, 1922

I am a man of limited talent from a small town.
I don't seem to grasp that I am President.

WARREN G. HARDING

That's where we gotta cut our losses. My losses are
to be cut. The President's losses gotta be cut on the
cover-up deal.

RICHARD M. NIXON, 1973

There can be no whitewash at the White House.
RICHARD M. NIXON, 1973


The first test of a truly great man is his humility.
RUSKIN
*Modern Painters*, 1843–60

Put a rogue in the limelight and he will act like an
honest man.
NAPOLEON BONAPARTE
*Maxims*, 1804–15

The errors of great men are venerable because they
are more fruitful than the truths of little men.
NIETZSCHE
"Fragment of a Critique of Schopenhauer", 1867

Power is the ultimate aphrodisiac.
HENRY KISSINGER


Every great action is extreme . . .
STENDHAL
*The Red and the Black*, 1830


A prince also wins prestige for being a true friend
or a true enemy, that is, for revealing himself
without any reservation in favour of one side
against another. This policy is always more
advantageous than neutrality.
MACHIAVELLI
*The Prince*, 1513

I don't give a shit what happens. I want you all to
stonewall it. Let them plead the Fifth Amendment,
cover up, or anything else if it'll save the plan.
RICHARD M. NIXON, 1973

He that humbleth himself wishes to be exalted.
NIETZSCHE<br>*Human, All Too Human,* 1878

I let down my friends, I let down my country.
I let down our system of government.
RICHARD M. NIXON, 1977

The great are great only because we are on our
knees.

PROUDHON

The will to power ... far from being a
characteristic of the strong, is, like envy and greed,
among the vices of the weak, and possibly their
most dangerous one.
HANNAH ARENDT

One will seldom go wrong if one attributes extreme
actions to vanity ...
NIETZSCHE<br>*Beyond Good and Evil,* 1886

I must follow them; I am their leader.
ANDREW BONAR LAW

What is it that every man seeks? To be secure, to be happy, to do what he pleases without restraint and without compulsion.
EPICTETUS
*Discourses*, 1st century A.D.

None who have always been free can understand the terrible fascinating power of the hope of freedom to those who are not free.
PEARL S. BUCK
*What America Means to Me*, 1943

Lean liberty is better than fat slavery.
THOMAS FULLER
*Gnomologia*, 1732

I know not what course others may take, but as for me, give me liberty or give me death!
PATRICK HENRY, 1775

To renounce liberty is to renounce being a man, to surrender the rights of humanity and even its duties.
ROUSSEAU
*The Social Contract*, 1762

Diversity of opinion is the essence of freedom.
LORD DEVLIN, 1967

The job of a citizen is to keep his mouth open.
GÜNTER GRASS, 1965

Liberty is the right to do what the laws permit.
MONTESQUIEU
*L'Esprit des Lois*, 1748

Freedom is the will to be responsible to ourselves.
NIETZSCHE
*Twilight of the Idols*, 1889

Liberty is so much latitude as the powerful choose
to accord to the weak.

JUDGE LEARNED HAND, 1930

Freedom's just another word for nothing left to
lose.

KRIS KRISTOFFERSON<br>"Me and Bobby McGee"

The hungry and the homeless don't care about
liberty any more than they care about cultural
heritage. To pretend that they do care is cant.

E. M. FORSTER<br>Abinger Harvest, 1936

Most people want security in this world, not
liberty.

H. L. MENCKEN<br>Minority Report, 1956

What men value in this world is not rights, but
privileges.

H. L. MENCKEN<br>Minority Report, 1956

Liberty is conforming to the majority.

HUGH SCANLON, 1977

The right to be heard does not automatically
include the right to be taken seriously.

HUBERT HUMPHREY, 1965

Liberty is the right to tell people what they do not
want to hear.

GEORGE ORWELL, 1945

It's often safer to be in chains than to be free.

FRANZ KAFKA<br>The Trial, 1925

# Life

To live is to be slowly born.
SAINT-EXUPÉRY
*Flight to Arras*, 1942

Since it is not granted to us to live long, let us
transmit to posterity some memorial that we have
at least lived.
PLINY THE YOUNGER
*Letters, c.* A.D. 97–110

The best thing for a man to do is to be born and,
being born, to die at once.
PIETRO ARETINO, 1537

Life is just a bowl of cherries.
LEW BROWN

Life is a jest, and all things show it; I thought so
once, but now I know it.
JOHN GAY
*Fables*, 1727

Life is a maze in which we take the wrong turning
before we have learned to walk.
CYRIL CONNOLLY
*The Unquiet Grave*, 1944

I dance to the tune that is played.
Spanish proverb

The world is not what it purports to be, but it has
no other meaning.
EDWARD GOREY, 1976

Man always dies before he is fully born.

ERICH FROMM
*Man for Himself*, 1947

A man dies still if he has done nothing, as one who
has done much.

HOMER
*Iliad*, 8th century B.C.

It is nothing to die; it is frightful not to live.

VICTOR HUGO
*Les Misérables*, 1862

Life is rather like a tin of sardines – we're all of us
looking for the key.

ALAN BENNETT
*Beyond the Fringe*

Life was a damned muddle . . . a football game with
everyone off-side and the referee gotten rid of . . .

F. SCOTT FITZGERALD
*This Side of Paradise*, 1920

The actual tragedies of life bear no relation to one's
preconceived ideas. In the event, one is always
bewildered by their simplicity, their grandeur of
design, and by that element of the bizarre which
seems inherent in them.

JEAN COCTEAU
*Les Enfants Terribles*, 1929

I thought life was going to be like Brahms, do you
know? Instead it's well it's been Eric Coates. And
very nice too. But not Brahms.

ALAN BENNETT
*Getting On*, 1974

Is not the whole world a vast house of assignation
to which the filing system has been lost?

QUENTIN CRISP
*The Naked Civil Servant*, 1968

Adapt or perish, now as ever, is Nature's
inexorable imperative.
H. G. WELLS
*Mind at the End of its Tether*, 1944


Man's main task in life is to give birth to himself.
ERICH FROMM
*Man for Himself*, 1947


Human life is mainly a process of filling in time
until the arrival of death or Santa Claus . . .
ERIC BERNE
*Games People Play*, 1964


Cruelty is the law pervading all nature and society;
and we can't get out of it if we would.
THOMAS HARDY
*Jude the Obscure*, 1895


Life's a pudding full of plums.
W. S. GILBERT
*The Gondoliers*, 1889


The aim of life is to live, and to live means to be
aware, joyously, drunkenly, serenely, divinely
aware.
HENRY MILLER
*The Wisdom of the Heart*, 1941


Life is an end in itself, and the only question as to
whether it is worth living is whether you have
enough of it.
OLIVER WENDELL HOLMES, 1900


Life is a tragedy when seen close-up, but a comedy
in long shot.
CHARLIE CHAPLIN

The supple, well-adjusted man is the one who has
learned to hop into the meat-grinder while
humming a hit-parade tune.

MARSHALL MCLUHAN
*The Mechanical Bride*, 1951

There is no cure for birth and death, save to enjoy
the interval.

GEORGE SANTAYANA
*Soliloquies in England*, 1922

No never forget! ... Never forget any moment;
they are too few.

ELIZABETH BOWEN
*To the North*, 1932

One's cruelty is one's power; and when one parts
with one's cruelty, one parts with one's power;
and when one has parted with that, I fancy one is
old and ugly.

WILLIAM CONGREVE
*The Way of the World*, 1700

Life is like an onion, which one peels crying.

French proverb

Life is a progress from want to want, not from
enjoyment to enjoyment.

SAMUEL JOHNSON
in Boswell, *Life of Johnson*, 1791

Obsessed by a fairly-tale, we spend our lives
searching for a magic door and a lost kingdom of
peace.

EUGENE O'NEILL
*More Stately Mansions*, 1964

Life is like a B-picture script. It is that corny. If I
had my life story offered to me to film, I'd turn it
down.

KIRK DOUGLAS, 1955

How good is man's life, the mere living! how fit to
employ / All the heart and the soul and the senses
forever in joy!
ROBERT BROWNING
"Saul", 1855

Whoever is not in his coffin and the dark grave let
him know he has enough.
WALT WHITMAN
*Leaves of Grass*, 1855–92


The time of life is short! / To spend that shortness
basely were too long.
SHAKESPEARE
*I Henry IV*, 1597–8

We love life, not because we are used to living but
because we are used to loving.
NIETZSCHE
*Thus Spake Zarathustra*, 1883–92

Life is short, but its ills make it seem long.
PUBLILIUS SYRUS
*Moral Sayings*, 1st century B.C.

Life, as it is called, is for most of us one long
postponement.

HENRY MILLER
*The Wisdom of the Heart*, 1941

Deem not life a thing of consequence. For look at
the yawning void of the future, and at that other
limitless space, the past.

MARCUS AURELIUS
*Meditations*, 2nd century A.D.

Man pines to live but cannot endure the days of his
life.

EDWARD DAHLBERG
*The Sorrows of Priapus*, 1957

Of all human foibles love of living is the most
powerful.

MOLIÈRE
*L'Amour Médecin*, 1665

Life is seldom as unendurable as, to judge by the
facts, it logically ought to be.

BROOKS ATKINSON
*Once Around the Sun*, 1951

# Love

Love is the only effective counter to death.
MAUREEN DUFFY
*Wounds*, 1969


They say falling in love is wonderful / It's
wonderful so they say.
IRVING BERLIN
"Falling in Love"


To fear love is to fear life, and those who fear life
are already three parts dead.
BERTRAND RUSSELL
*Marriage and Morals*, 1929


Love is not the dying moan of a distant violin – it is
the triumphant twang of a bedspring.
S. J. PERELMAN


I know of only one duty, and that is to love.
ALBERT CAMUS
*The Notebooks 1935–42*, 1962


The only abnormality is the incapacity to love.
ANAÏS NIN


One must not be mean with the affections, what is
spent of the fund is renewed in the spending itself.
SIGMUND FREUD, 1882


Absence makes the heart grow fonder.
English proverb


If an individual is able to love productively, he
loves himself too; if he can love *only* others, he
cannot love at all.
ERICH FROMM
*The Art of Loving*, 1956

# Love

Love is only the dirty trick played on us to achieve
continuation of the species.

> W. SOMERSET MAUGHAM
> *A Writer's Notebook*, 1949

Love . . . is the extremely difficult realization that
something other than oneself is real.

> IRIS MURDOCH, 1968

We have to distrust each other. It is our only
defense against betrayal.

> TENNESSEE WILLIAMS
> *Camino Real*, 1953

How alike are the groans of love to those of the
dying.

> MALCOLM LOWRY
> *Under the Volcano*, 1947

What we need is hatred – from it our ideas are
born.

> JEAN GENET
> *The Blacks*, 1960

Sometimes I wish I could fall in love. Then at least
you know who your opponent is.

> PETER USTINOV
> *Romanoff and Juliet*, 1957

I can understand companionship. I can
understand bought sex in the afternoon. I cannot
understand the love affair.

> GORE VIDAL, 1973

What the eye sees not, the heart craves not.

> Dutch proverb

When love gets to be important to someone, it
means that he hasn't been able to manage
something else.

> RICHARD G. STERN

Jealousy: that dragon which slays love under the
pretense of keeping it alive.
HAVELOCK ELLIS
*On Life and Sex: Essays of Love and Virtue*, 1937

Jealousy is the greatest of all evils . . .
LA ROCHEFOUCAULD
*Maxims*, 1665

To love without role, without power plays, is
revolution.
RITA MAE BROWN, 1970

The important thing is not to let oneself be
poisoned. Now, hatred poisons.
ANDRÉ GIDE
*The Journal*, 1939

Rather perish than hate and fear . . .
NIETZSCHE

One cannot be strong without love.
PAUL TILLICH
*The Eternal Now*, 1963

Where there is no jealousy there is no love.

German proverb


Jealousy is not at all low, but it catches us humbled
and bowed down, at first sight.

COLETTE
*Earthly Paradise*, 1966

Is it better to be the lover or the loved one? Neither,
if your cholesterol is over six hundred.

WOODY ALLEN
*Without Feathers*, 1972

I find just as much profit in cultivating my hates as
my love.

ANDRÉ GIDE
*The Journal*, 1939

Now Hatred is by far the longest pleasure; / Men
love in haste, but they detest at leisure.

BYRON
*Don Juan*, 1819–24

Love is simple to understand if you haven't got a
mind full of holes. It's a crutch, that's all . . .

NORMAN MAILER
*Barbary Shore*, 1951

# Marriage

The one point on which all women are in furious
secret rebellion against the existing law is the
saddling of the right to a child with the obligation
to become the servant of a man.
GEORGE BERNARD SHAW
*Getting Married*, 1911

Marriage is the deep, deep peace of the double bed
after the hurly-burly of the chaise longue.
MRS PATRICK CAMPBELL

Familiarity breeds contentment.
GEORGE ADE
*Hand-Made Fables*, 1920

What therefore God hath joined together, let not
man put asunder.
Matthew 19:6

Those marriages generally abound most with love
and constancy that are preceded by a long
courtship. The passion should strike root and
gather strength before marriage be grafted on it.
JOSEPH ADDISON
*The Spectator*, 1711–12

It is not the seven deadly virtues that makes a man
a good husband, but the three hundred pleasing
amiabilities.
W. SOMERSET MAUGHAM
*The Constant Wife*, 1927

Our marriage is dead, when pleasure is fled: /
'Twas pleasure first made it an oath.
DRYDEN
*Songs*, 1673

The happy married man dies in good stile at home,
surrounded by his weeping wife and children. The
old bachelor don't die at all – he sort of rots away…
ARTEMUS WARD
*Artemus Ward, His Book*, 1862

All any woman asks of her husband is that he love
her and obey her commandments.

JOHN W. ROPER

Marriage is a great institution, but I'm not ready
for an institution, yet.

MAE WEST

Though familiarity may not breed contempt, it
takes off the edge of admiration.

WILLIAM HAZLITT<br>*Characteristics*, 1823

There are four stages to a marriage. First there's
the affair, then the marriage, then children and
finally the fourth stage, without which you cannot
know a woman, the divorce.

NORMAN MAILER, 1969

Courtship to marriage is as a very witty prologue
to a very dull play.

WILLIAM CONGREVE<br>*The Old Batchelor*, 1693

In marriage, a man becomes slack and selfish, and
undergoes a fatty degeneration of his moral being.

R. L. STEVENSON<br>*Virginibus Puerisque*, 1881

A difference of taste in jokes is a great strain on the
affections.

GEORGE ELIOT<br>*Daniel Deronda*, 1874–6

Better is the end of a thing than the beginning
thereof.

Ecclesiasticus 7:8

If you are human you love and doubt. The only
thing there shouldn't be any doubt about is your
wife. If there is, it's finished.
MARC CHAGALL


A man's friend loves him but leaves him as he is:
his wife loves him and is always trying to turn him
into something else.
G. K. CHESTERTON
*Orthodoxy*, 1908


A happy marriage is a long conversation which
always seems too short.
ANDRÉ MAUROIS
*Memories*, 1970


I shall marry in haste and repeat at leisure.
JAMES BRANCH CABELL


# Medicine


To preserve a man alive in the midst of so many
chances and hostilities, is as great a miracle as to
create him.
JEREMY TAYLOR
*The Rule and Exercise of Holy Dying*, 1651


Men who are occupied in the restoration of health
to other men, by the joint exertion of skill and
humanity, are above all the great of the earth.
They even partake of divinity, since to preserve
and renew is almost as noble as to create.
VOLTAIRE
*Philosophical Dictionary*, 1764


We have not lost faith, but we have transferred it
from God to the medical profession.
GEORGE BERNARD SHAW

Men are always doomed to be duped ... They are always wooing goddesses, and marrying mere mortals.

WASHINGTON IRVING<br>*Bracebridge Hall,* 1822

Most women set out to try to change man, and when they have changed him they do not like him.

MARLENE DIETRICH

A man is in general better pleased when he has a good dinner upon his table, than when his wife talks Greek.

SAMUEL JOHNSON

A man in love is incomplete until he is married. Then he is finished.

ZSA ZSA GABOR, 1960

# Medicine

God heals, and the doctor takes the fees.

BENJAMIN FRANKLIN<br>*Poor Richard's Almanack,* 1732–57

There is a sort of decency among the dead, a remarkable discretion: you never find them making any complaint against the doctor who killed them!

MOLIÈRE<br>*Le Médecin Malgré Lui,* 1666

Only a fool will make a doctor his heir.

Russian proverb

The best doctor in the world is the veterinarian. He can't ask his patients what is the matter – he's got to just know.
WILL ROGERS
*The Autobiography of Will Rogers*, 1949

As long as men are liable to die and desirous to live, physicians will be made fun of but well paid.
LA BRUYÈRE
*Characters*, 1688

Wherever the art of medicine is loved, there also is love of humanity.
HIPPOCRATES, 5th–4th centuries B.C.

Doctors are the guardians of our bodies, as priests, ministers and rabbis are the guardians of our souls. Doctors try to keep us from the heaven or hell that the priests, ministers and rabbis promise.
DR OSCAR FASKER

It is medicine, not scenery, for which a sick man must go searching.
SENECA
*Letters to Lucilius*, 1st century A.D.

Who ever saw one physician approve of another's prescription, without subtracting something from, or adding something to it?
MONTAIGNE
*Essays*, 1580–88

However complete the conspiracy of silence about the blunders and failures of medicine may be, the really scientific doctors and biologists know about them and cannot rest until they find out what is wrong with them.
GEORGE BERNARD SHAW
*Everybody's Political What's What?*, 1944

Oh, the powers of nature! She knows what we
need, and the doctors know nothing.

BENVENUTO CELLINI
*Autobiography*, 1558–66

Keep away from physicians. It is all probing and
guessing and pretending with them. They leave it
to Nature to cure in her own time, but they take
the credit. As well as very fat fees.

ANTHONY BURGESS
*Nothing Like The Sun*, 1964

Let no one suppose that the words doctor and
patient can disguise from the parties the fact that
they are employer and employee.

GEORGE BERNARD SHAW
*The Doctor's Dilemma*, 1913

The general order of things, that takes care of fleas
and moles, also takes care of men if they will have
the patience to leave it to itself.

MONTAIGNE
*Essays*, 1580–88

The best doctors in the world are Doctor Diet,
Doctor Quiet, and Doctor Merryman.

JONATHAN SWIFT
*Polite Conversation*, 1738

Keep a watch also on the faults of the patients,
which often make them lie about taking things
that were prescribed.

HIPPOCRATES
*Decorum, c.* 400 B.C.

It is idle to declare that we have, in the honour of a
noble profession, a psychological guarantee
against medical corruption.

GEORGE BERNARD SHAW
*Everybody's Political What's What?*, 1944

God is not a man
Numbers 23:19


I must have women. There is nothing unbends the
mind like them.
JOHN GAY
*The Beggar's Opera*, 1728


There be three things which are too wonderful for
me, / Yea, four which I know not: / The way of an
eagle in the air; / The way of a serpent upon a
rock; / The way of a ship in the midst of the sea; /
And the way of a man with a maid.
Proverbs 30:18–19


Woman is woman's natural ally.
EURIPIDES
*Alope*, 5th century B.C.


Forgetting is woman's first and greatest art.
RICHARD ALDINGTON
*The Colonel's Daughter*, 1931


Disguise our bondage as we will, / 'Tis woman,
woman, rules us still.
THOMAS MOORE
"Sovereign Woman"


Women never reason, and therefore they are
(comparatively) seldom wrong.
WILLIAM HAZLITT
*Characteristics*, 1823


If women didn't exist, all the money in the world
would have no meaning.
ARISTOTLE ONASSIS

The gods are come down to us in the likeness of men.

Acts 14:11

Of all the plagues with which the world is curst, Of every ill, a woman is the worst.

GEORGE GRANVILLE
"The British Enchanters", 1706

With many women I doubt whether there be any more effectual way of touching their hearts than ill-using them ... If you wish to get the sweetest fragrance from the herb at your feet, tread on it and bruise it.

TROLLOPE
*Miss Mackenzie*, 1865

The woman is so hard / Upon the woman.

TENNYSON
*The Princess*, 1847

Women and elephants never forget an injury.

SAKI (H. H. MUNRO)
*Reginald*, 1904

Man is the hunter; woman is his game: / the sleek and shining creatures of the chase, / We hunt them for the beauty of their skins; / They love us for it, and we ride them down.

TENNYSON
*The Princess*, 1847

A woman's guess is much more accurate than a man's certainty.

KIPLING
*Plain Tales from the Hills*, 1888

I could not possibly count the gold-digging ruses of women, / Not if I had ten mouths, not if I had ten tongues.

OVID
*The Art of Love*, A.D. 8

Wommen desiren to have sovereynetee / As well
over hir husband as hir love.
CHAUCER
*The Wife of Bath's Tale*, c. 1387

But what is woman? – only one of nature's
agreeable blunders.
MRS HANNAH COWLEY
*Who's the Dupe?*, 1779

Woman is the lesser man, and all thy passions
match'd with mine, / Are as moonlight unto
sunlight, and as water unto wine.
TENNYSON
"Locksley Hall", 1842

Woman loves or hates: she knows no middle
course.
PUBLILIUS SYRUS
*Moral Sayings*, 1st century B.C.

There is in every true woman's heart a spark of
heavenly fire, which lies dormant in the broad
daylight of prosperity, but which kindles up and
beams and blazes in the dark hour of adversity.
WASHINGTON IRVING
*The Sketch Book of Geoffrey Crayon, Gent.*, 1819–20

A thoroughly beautiful woman and a thoroughly
homely woman are creations which I love to gaze
upon, and which I cannot tire of gazing upon, for
each is perfect in her own line.
MARK TWAIN
*Autobiography*, 1924

Women, then, are only children of a larger
growth: they have an entertaining tattle, and
sometimes wit; but for solid, reasoning good-sense,
I never knew in my life one that had it, or who
reasoned or acted consequentially for four and
twenty hours together.
LORD CHESTERFIELD
*Letters to His Son*, 1774

I do not wish them to have power over men, but
over themselves.

MARY WOLLSTONECRAFT
*A Vindication of the Rights of Women*, 1792

I'm not denyin' the women are foolish: God
Almighty made 'em to match the men.

GEORGE ELIOT
*Adam Bede*, 1859

A man's women folk, whatever their outward
show of respect for his merit and authority, always
regard him secretly as an ass, and with something
akin to pity.

H. L. MENCKEN
*In Defense of Women*, 1922

If women got a slap round the face more often,
they'd be a bit more reasonable.

CHARLOTTE RAMPLING, 1983

There are only three things to be done with a
woman. You can love her, suffer for her, or turn
her into literature.

LAWRENCE DURRELL
*Justine*, 1957

Is it too much to ask that women be spared the
daily struggle for superhuman beauty in order to
offer it to the caresses of a subhumanly ugly mate?

GERMAINE GREER
*The Female Eunuch*, 1970

Men are but children of a larger growth, / Our
appetites as apt to change as theirs, / And full as
craving too, and full as vain.

DRYDEN
"All For Love," 1678

Women have many faults, / Men have only two – /
Everything they say and / Everything they do
graffito


It is not good that the man should be alone; I will
make him an help meet for him.
Genesis, 2:18


A man is like a phonograph with half-a-dozen
records. You soon get tired of them all; and yet you
have to sit at table whilst he reels them off to every
new visitor.
GEORGE BERNARD SHAW
*Getting Married*, 1911

Poor little men! Poor little strutting peacocks!
They spread out their tails as conquerors almost as
soon as they are able to walk.
JEAN ANOUILH
*Cécile*, 1949

*Male.* n. A member of the unconsidered or
negligible sex ... commonly known (to the female)
as Mere Man.
AMBROSE BIERCE
*The Devil's Dictionary*, 1881–1911

Our Aunts and Grandmothers allwaies tell us Men
are a sort of Animals, that if ever they are constant
'tis only where they are ill-us'd ... Experience has
taught me the truth of it.
LADY MARY WORTLEY MONTAGU
*The Complete Letters 1708–62*

Women have simple tastes. They can get pleasure
out of the conversation of children in arms and
men in love.
H. L. MENCKEN
*A Book of Burlesques*, 1920

Women are much more like each other than men: they have, in truth, but two passions, vanity and love; these are their universal characteristics.

LORD CHESTERFIELD
*Letters to His Son*, 1774

God created man and, finding him not sufficiently alone, gave him a companion to make him feel his solitude more keenly.

PAUL VALÉRY
*Tel quel*, 1943

Women are a decorative sex. They never have anything to say, but they say it charmingly.

OSCAR WILDE
*The Picture of Dorian Gray*, 1891

Women are one and all a set of vultures.

PETRONIUS
*Satyricon*, 1st century A.D.

Let *Greeks* be *Greeks*, and women what they are, /
Men have precedency, and still excell.

ANNE BRADSTREET
"The Prologue", *The Tenth Muse* . . . , 1650

Certain women should be struck regularly, like gongs.

NOËL COWARD
*Private Lives*, 1930

Women are never stronger than when they arm themselves with their weaknesses

MARQUISE DU DEFFAND
*Letters to Voltaire*, 1759–75

# Monarchy

Fear created gods; audacity created kings.
CRÉBILLON *père*
*Xerxes*, 1714

A monarch frequently represents his subjects
better than an elected assembly; and if he is a good
judge of character he is likely to have more capable
and loyal advisers.
DEAN INGE
*Outspoken Essays: First Series*, 1919

'Twixt kings and tyrants there's this difference
known; / Kings seek their subjects' good, tyrants
their own.
ROBERT HERRICK
"Kings and Tyrants", 1648

I think it is a perfectly valid system of producing a
head of state. It's been very successful for 1,000
years. It's had its ups and downs, undoubtedly.
PRINCE PHILIP

The monarchy system adds gaiety to politics.
PRINCE PHILIP

The characteristic of the English monarchy is that
it retains the feeling by which the heroic kings
governed their rude age, and has added the feeling
by which the constitutions of later Greece ruled in
more refined ages.
WALTER BAGEHOT
*The English Constitution*, 1867

The British monarchical system is the highest
pinnacle of achievement in the ordering of human
affairs and without doubt it is our destiny to
protect and nurture it and keep it as an example to
the world.
BRIGADIER RICHARD EASON, head of the British
Brotherhood, Australia

A king can stand people's fighting but he can't last long if people start thinking.

WILL ROGERS
*The Autobiography of Will Rogers*, 1949

All kings is mostly rapscallions.

MARK TWAIN
*The Adventures of Huckleberry Finn*, 1884

Kings will be tyrants from policy, when subjects are rebels from principle.

EDMUND BURKE
*Reflections on the Revolution in France*, 1790

My objection to the Royal symbol is that it is dead; it is a gold filling in a mouth full of decay. When the mobs rush forward in the Mall they are taking part in the last circus of a civilization that has lost faith in itself and sold itself for a splendid triviality.

JOHN OSBORNE

We don't need a royal circus. We need roads, industry, schools, indoor lavatories and water laid on.

DAFYDD IWAN

The kingly office is entitled to no respect. It was originally procured by highwayman's methods; it remains a perpetuated crime, can never be anything but the symbol of a crime. It is no more entitled to respect than is the flag of a pirate.

MARK TWAIN
*Notebook*, 1935

The continuous brainwashing of the plebs in the schools and the churches and the Press and on television and radio creates an atmosphere of adoring stupefaction. As a nation we have forsaken God for Elizabeth II, with Prince Philip as a latterday John the Baptist.

WILLIE HAMILTON

# Music

Except for theology, there is no art that can be
placed in comparison with music.
MARTIN LUTHER
*Letters*, 1530–41

Music . . . can name the unnamable and
communicate the unknowable.
LEONARD BERNSTEIN
*The Unanswered Question*, 1976

The art of conducting lies . . . in the power of
suggestion that the conductor exerts, on the
audience as well as on the orchestra.
OTTO KLEMPERER, 1973

Mozart is the human incarnation of the divine
force of creation.
GOETHE

A taste of sculpture and painting is in my mind as
becoming as a taste of fiddling and piping is
unbecoming a man of fashion. The former is
connected with history and poetry, the latter, with
nothing that I know of but bad company.
LORD CHESTERFIELD, 1749

Music is a roaring-meg against melancholy, to rear
and revive the languishing soul; affecting not only
the ears, but the very arteries, the vital and animal
spirits, it erects the mind and makes it nimble.
BURTON
*Anatomy of Melancholy*, 1621

Music is the imagination of love in *sound*. It is what
man imagines of his life, and his life is love.
W. J. TURNER
*Orpheus, or The Music of the Future*, 1926

# Music

A great fondness for music is a mark of great weakness, great vacuity of mind: not of hardness of heart; not of vice; not of downright folly; but of a want of capacity, or inclination, for sober thought.

WILLIAM COBBETT
*Advice to Young Men* etc., 1829–30

The plain fact is that music *per se* means nothing; it is sheer sound . . .

SIR THOMAS BEECHAM
*A Mingled Chime*, 1973

Conducting is a real sport. You can never guarantee what the results are going to be so there's always an element of chance. That's what keeps it exciting.

AARON COPLAND, 1978

I write as a sow pisses.

MOZART

If I were to begin life again, I would devote much time to music. All musical people seem to me happy; it is the most engrossing pursuit, almost the only innocent and unpunished passion.

SYDNEY SMITH, *c.* 1840

Music is essentially useless, as life is.

GEORGE SANTAYANA
*Little Essays*, 1920

. . . music is the brandy of the damned.

GEORGE BERNARD SHAW
*Man and Superman*, 1903

When we separate music from life, we get art.
JOHN CAGE
*Silence,* 1961


Music is, by its very nature, essentially powerless
to express anything at all . . . music expresses itself.
IGOR STRAVINSKY, 1972


Those things that act through the ears are said to
make a noise, discord, or harmony, and this last
has caused men to lose their heads to such a
degree that they have believed God himself is
delighted with it.
SPINOZA
*Ethics,* 1677

Rock 'n' roll is the most brutal, ugly, vicious form
of expression – sly, lewd, in fact plain dirty. . . .
FRANK SINATRA, 1957

New music: new listening. Not an attempt to
understand something that is being said, for, if
something were being said, the sounds would be
given the shapes of words. Just an attention to the
activity of sounds.
JOHN CAGE
*Silence,* 1961

Nothing is more futile than theorizing about
music.

HEINE
*Letters on the French Stage*, 1837

There never was a more imbecile notion than the
twentieth-century cult of Pure Music, for the
simple reason that although in one sense all music
must be programme music, since it is concerned
with human emotions, in another sense music, in
so far as it *is* music, can never be anything but
pure.

W. H. MELLARS
"The Textual Criticism of Music", 1939

A carpenter's hammer, in a warm summer noon,
will fret me into more than midsummer madness.
But those unconnected, unset sounds are nothing
to the measured malice of music.

CHARLES LAMB
*Essays of Elia*, 1823

I don't know anything about music. In my line you
don't have to.

ELVIS PRESLEY

I occasionally play works by contemporary
composers and for two reasons. First to discourage
the composer from writing any more and secondly
to remind myself how much I appreciate
Beethoven.

JASCHA HEIFETZ

# Old age

It is better to wear out than to rust out.
Proverb


People are too durable, that's their main trouble.
They can do too much to themselves, they last too
long.
BERTOLT BRECHT
*Jungle of Cities*, 1924

The joy of being older is that in one's life one can,
towards the end of the run, over-act appallingly.
QUENTIN CRISP, 1981

Age only matters when one is ageing. Now that I
have arrived at a great age, I might just as well be
twenty.
PABLO PICASSO

The advantage of being eighty years old is that one
has had many people to love.
JEAN RENOIR


There is no such thing as "on the way out". As
long as you are still doing something interesting
and good, you're in business because you're still
breathing.
LOUIS ARMSTRONG, 1969

To grow old is to pass from passion to compassion.
ALBERT CAMUS


The passing years steal from us one thing after
another.
HORACE
*Epistles*, 20–8 B.C.

When I was young, I was told: "You'll see, when
you're fifty." I am fifty and I haven't seen a thing.
ERIK SATIE

# Old age

Better to be eaten to death with a rust than to be scoured to nothing with perpetual motion.

SHAKESPEARE
*Henry IV*, 1600

Old age isn't so bad when you consider the alternative.

MAURICE CHEVALIER, 1960

Old age is life's parody.

SIMONE DE BEAUVOIR
*The Coming of Age*, 1972

Age is an ugly thing, and it goes on getting worse.

LADY DIANA COOPER

If you live long enough, you'll see that every victory turns into a defeat.

SIMONE DE BEAUVOIR
*Tous les Hommes Sont Mortels*, 1947

The role of a retired person is no longer to possess one.

SIMONE DE BEAUVOIR
*The Coming of Age*, 1972

Chastity is not chastity in an old man but a disability to be chaste.

JOHN DONNE

To be without some of the things you want is an indispensable part of happiness.

BERTRAND RUSSELL
*The Conquest of Happiness*, 1930

Time strips our illusions of their hue. / And one by one in turn, some grand mistake / Casts off its bright skin yearly like the snake.

BYRON
*Don Juan*, 1819–24

At twenty man is a peacock, at thirty a lion, at
forty a camel, at fifty a serpent, at sixty a dog, at
seventy an ape, at eighty nothing at all.
BALTASAR GRACIÁN
*The Art of Worldly Wisdom*, 1647


The older I grow the more I distrust the familiar
doctrine that age brings wisdom.
H. L. MENCKEN


The notion that as a man grows older his illusions
leave him is not quite true. What is true is that his
early illusions are supplanted by new, and to him,
equally convincing illusions.
GEORGE JEAN NATHAN
*The Theatre, The Drama and Girls*, 1921


# Opera

If the inhabitant of another planet should visit the
earth, he would receive, on the whole, a truer
notion of human life by attending an Italian opera
than he would by reading Emerson's volumes. He
would learn from the Italian opera that there were
two sexes; and this, after all, is probably the fact
with which the education of such a stranger ought
to begin.
JOHN JAY CHAPMAN
*Emerson and Other Essays*, 1898


There is a childlike, unsophisticated quality about
opera which commands respect in this wicked
world. All that hooting and hollering because
somebody has pinched somebody else's girl, or
killed the wrong man, or sold his soul to the devil!
ROBERTSON DAVIES
*The Table Talk of Samuel Marchbanks*, 1949

The four stages of man are infancy, childhood,
adolescence and obsolescence.

ART LINKLETTER<br>
A Child's Garden of Misinformation, 1965


It has been said that there is no fool like an old fool,
except a young fool. But the young fool has first to
grow up to be an old fool to realize what a damn
fool he was when he was a young fool.

HAROLD MACMILLAN


I hope to die before I get old.

PETE TOWNSHEND<br>
"Substitute"


# Opera


I don't really believe in it. You know, how can
people sing away their troubles? How can they all
make love to each other singing ... ?

JOSE QUINTERO


... a rudimentary redundancy in grand opera as
exemplified in simultaneously showing a sword on
the stage, speaking about a sword in the book,
singing about a sword, and introducing a pre-
arranged labelled sword motive in the orchestral
part?

WALFORD DAVIES<br>
The Pursuit of Music, 1944

Opera is the most highly developed and complete
form of art in music, and to sing in opera should be
the aim of every vocalist. All vocal performance
should be dramatised and opera should be the goal
of every composer. And the utility of concerts should
be to train audiences and all concerned for opera.
SIR THOMAS BEECHAM

I think my favourite opera of all is *Die
Meistersinger*, and I have always thought that I
would like to die to the strains of the last act but
one to that. Lovely music, enchanting music.
W. SOMERSET MAUGHAM

It is the best of all trades, to make songs, and the
second best to sing them.
HILAIRE BELLOC
*On Everything*, 1909

# Optimism & Pessimism

The optimist thinks that this is the best of all
possible worlds and the pessimist knows it.
J. ROBERT OPPENHEIMER, 1951

He who despairs over an event is a coward, but he
who holds hopes for the human condition is a fool.
ALBERT CAMUS
*The Notebooks*, 1962

I came to the conclusion that the optimist thought
everything good except the pessimist, and that the
pessimist thought everything bad, except himself.
G. K. CHESTERTON
*Orthodoxy*, 1908

People are inexterminable – like flies and bedbugs.
There will always be some that survive in cracks
and crevices – that's us.
ROBERT FROST, 1959

There was a time when I heard eleven operas in a
fortnight ... which left me bankrupt and half-
idiotic for a month.

J. B. PRIESTLEY<br>
"All About Ourselves", 1923

Wagner has some wonderful moments but awful
half hours.

ROSSINI

For my part, I am convinced that people applaud a
prima donna as they do the feats of the strong man
at a fair. The sensations are painfully disagreeable,
hard to endure, but one is so glad when it is all
over that one cannot help rejoicing.

ROUSSEAU<br>
*La Nouvelle Héloïse*, 1761

# Optimism & Pessimism

Life is divided into the horrible and the miserable.

WOODY ALLEN<br>
*Annie Hall*

One must choose in life between boredom and
torment.

MME DE STAËL, 1800

Do you know what a pessimist is? A man who
thinks everybody is as nasty as himself and hates
himself for it.

GEORGE BERNARD SHAW

As an archaeology of our thought easily shows,
man is an invention of recent date. And one
perhaps nearing its end.

MICHEL FOUCAULT<br>
*The Order of Things*, 1970

There may be trouble ahead / But while there's
moonlight, and music, and love, and romance /
Let's face the music and dance.
IRVING BERLIN
"Let's Face the Music and Dance", *Follow the Fleet*,
1936

The days that make us happy make us wise.
JOHN MASEFIELD

We can destroy ourselves by cynicism and
disillusion, just as effectively as by bombs.
LORD CLARK

Cynicism – the intellectual cripple's substitute for
intelligence.
RUSSELL LYNES

Don't you know each cloud contains / Pennies
from Heaven?
JOHNNY BURKE
"Pennies From Heaven"

He who laughs has not yet heard the bad news.
BERTOLT BRECHT

Modern man thinks he loses something – time –
when he does not do things quickly. Yet he does
not know what to do with the time he gains –
except kill it.
ERICH FROMM<br>*The Art of Loving*, 1956

Everything is worth precisely as much as a belch,
the difference being that the belch is more
satisfying.
INGMAR BERGMAN

Nothing matters very much and few things matter
at all.
ARTHUR BALFOUR

The light at the end of the tunnel is only the
headlight of the oncoming train.
anon

# Parents

Give a little love to a child, and you get a great deal
back.
RUSKIN
*The Crown of Wild Olive*, 1866


I'm jolly lucky, I've got a sensational nanny. I
can't really imagine life without a smashing
nanny. Otherwise you get totally bogged down in
the Earth Mother bit.
PATREA MORE NISBETT, 1982


Rejoice! Rejoice! And call your / Mother once in a
while.
WOODY ALLEN
*Without Feathers*, 1972


Romance fails us and so do friendships, but the
relationship of parent and child, less noisy than all
others, remains indelible and indestructible, the
strongest relationship on earth.
THEODOR REIK
*Of Love and Lust*, 1957


To make your children *capable of honesty* is the
beginning of education.
RUSKIN
*Time and Tide*, 1907


So for the mother's sake the child was dear
And dearer was the mother for the child.
S. T. COLERIDGE
"Sonnet to a Friend who Asked How I Felt When
the Nurse First Presented My Infant to Me", 1796



For a moment you have the strange feeling of
being double; but there is something more, quite
impossible to analyze – perhaps the echo in a
man's heart of all the sensations felt by all the
fathers and mothers of his race . . . It is a very
tender, but also a very ghostly feeling.
LAFCADIO HEARN

A child hasn't a grown-up person's appetite for affection. A little of it goes a long way with them; and they like a good imitation of it better than the real thing, as every nurse knows.

GEORGE BERNARD SHAW
*Getting Married*, 1911

Parents are the very last people who ought to be allowed to have children.

H. E. BELL, 1977

No woman can shake off her mother. There should be no mothers, only women.

GEORGE BERNARD SHAW
*Too Good to be True*

Children begin by loving their parents. After a time they judge them. Rarely, if ever, do they forgive them.

OSCAR WILDE
*A Woman of No Importance*, 1893

The best way to give advice to your children is to find out what they want and advise them to do it.

HARRY S. TRUMAN, 1955

From the moment of birth, when the Stone Age baby confronts the 20th-century mother, the baby is subjected to these forces of violence, called love, .... Those forces are mainly concerned with destroying most of its potentialities.

R. D. LAING
*The Politics of Experience*, 1967

Society moves by some degree of parricide, by which the children ... kill, if not their fathers, at least the beliefs of their fathers.

ISAIAH BERLIN, 1978

... father is needed at home to help mother to feel
well in her body and happy in her mind ... father
is needed to give mother moral support, to be the
backing for her authority, to be the human being
who stands for the law and order which mother
plants in the life of the child.
D. W. WINNICOTT
*The Child, the Family, and the Outside World*, 1964

Children are the anchors that hold a mother to life.
SOPHOCLES
*Phaedra*, c. 435–429 B.C.

The concept of "Momism" is male nonsense. It is
the refuge of a man seeking excuses for his own
lack of virility.
PEARL S. BUCK
*To My Daughters, with Love*, 1967

Perhaps a child who is fussed over gets a feeling of
destiny, he thinks he is in the world for something
important and it gives him drive and confidence.
BENJAMIN SPOCK, 1956

No man can possibly know what life means, what
the world means, what anything means, until he
has a child and loves it.
LAFCADIO HEARN
*Life and Letters*, 1906

I could not point to any need in childhood as
strong as a father's protection.
FREUD
*Civilization and its Discontents*, 1930

You have to dig deep to bury your father.
Gypsy proverb

It is known that a father is necessary, but not
known how to identify him, except negatively.
GERMAINE GREER<br>
The Female Eunuch, 1970

Schoolmasters and parents exist to be grown out
of.
JOHN WOLFENDEN, 1958

If a man smiles at home somebody is sure to ask
him for money.
WILLIAM FEATHER

They fuck you up, your mum and dad / They may
not mean to but they do / They fill you up with the
faults they had / And add some extra just for you.
PHILIP LARKIN<br>
"This be the Verse", High Windows, 1974

Children are cruel, ruthless, cunning and almost
incredibly self-centred. Far from cementing a
marriage children more frequently disrupt it.
Childrearing is on the whole an expensive and
unrewarding bore, in which more has to be
invested, both materially and spiritually, than ever
comes out in dividends.
NIGEL BALCHIN, 1965

I never could dance around you, my father ... As
soon as I left you, my father, the whole world
swung into a symphony.
ANAÏS NIN<br>
The Journals

There is no good father, that's the rule. Don't lay
the blame on men but on the bond of paternity,
which is rotten. To beget children, nothing better;
to have them, what iniquity.
JEAN-PAUL SARTRE<br>
Words, 1964

In every child who is born ... the potentiality of
the human race is born again; and in him too,
once more, and of each of us, our terrific
responsibility towards human life; towards the
utmost idea of goodness, of the horror of error, and
of God.
JAMES AGEE


... everyone who is sane, everyone who feels
himself to be a person in the world, and for whom
the world means something, every happy person,
is in infinite debt to a woman. At a time in earliest
infancy when there was no perception of
dependence, we were absolutely dependent.
D. W. WINNICOTT
*The Child, the Family and the Outside World*, 1964


To be a successful father, there's one absolute rule;
when you have a kid, don't look at it for the first
two years.
ERNEST HEMINGWAY


And, ye fathers, provoke not your children to
wrath.
Ephesians 6:4


I am trying to draw attention to the immense
contribution to the individual and to society which
the ordinary good mother with her husband in
support makes at the beginning, and which she
does *simply through being devoted to her infant*.
D. W. WINNICOTT
*The Child, the Family and the Outside World*, 1964

A son of my own! Oh, no, no, no! Let my flesh
perish with me, and let me not transmit to anyone
the boredom and the ignominiousness of life.

GUSTAVE FLAUBERT

Who has not watched a mother stroke her child's
cheek or kiss her child *in a certain way*, and felt a
nervous shudder at the passive outrage done to a
free solitary human soul.

JOHN COWPER POWYS
*The Meaning of Culture*, 1929

... on the whole, childhood seems all about love
and separation, love and longing, love and
rejection; a stupor of love unsatisfied; the
hopelessness of making oneself understood,
helplessly bombarded by incomprehensible pain,
the little comforts and jollities few and far between.

ELIZABETH SMART, 1981

In the old days you'd drag your old man out on the
lawn and kick the shit out of each other and he'd
say "Be home by midnight" and you'd be home by
midnight. Today parents daren't tell you what
time to be in. They're frightened you won't come
back.

FRANK ZAPPA

I love children. Especially when they cry – for then
someone takes them away.

NANCY MITFORD

# Patriotism

He who loves not his home and country which he
has seen, how shall he love humanity in general
which he has not seen?
DEAN INGE
*Outspoken Essays*, 1919

Our country! In her intercourse with foreign
nations may she always be in the right; but our
country, right or wrong.
STEPHEN DECATUR, 1779–1820

Ask not what your country can do for you: ask
what you can do for your country.
JOHN F. KENNEDY, 1961

Breathes there the man, with soul so dead, / Who
never to himself hath said, / This is my own, my
native land!
SIR WALTER SCOTT
*The Lay of the Last Minstrel*, 1805

What a pity is it / That we can die but once to save
our country!
ADDISON
*Cato*, 1713

I for one know of no sweeter sight for a man's eyes
than his own country.
HOMER
*Odyssey*, 9th century B.C.

Each blade of grass has its spot on earth whence it
draws its life, its strength; and so is man rooted to
the land from which he draws his faith together
with his life.
JOSEPH CONRAD
*Lord Jim*, 1900

Do we wish men to be virtuous? Then let us begin
by making them love their country.
ROUSSEAU
*Discourse on Political Economy*, 1758

# Patriotism

Nationalism is an infantile disease. It is the measles
of mankind.

ALBERT EINSTEIN
*The World As I See It*, 1935

We seek not the worldwide victory of one nation or
system but a worldwide victory of men.

JOHN F. KENNEDY, 1963

When a stupid man is doing something he is
ashamed of, he always declares that it is his duty.

GEORGE BERNARD SHAW
*Caesar and Cleopatra*, 1906

An author's first duty is to let down his country.

BRENDAN BEHAN, 1960

Patriotism is not a short and frenzied outburst of
emotion but the tranquil and steady dedication of
a lifetime.

ADLAI STEVENSON, 1952

Our true nationality is mankind.

H. G. WELLS
*The Outline of History*, 1920

I am a citizen of the world.

DIOGENES THE CYNIC, 4th century B.C.

If I had to choose between betraying my *country*
and betraying my *friend*, I hope I would have the
guts to betray my *country*.

E. M. FORSTER
*Two Cheers for Democracy*, 1951

Who saves his country violates no law.
NAPOLEON BONAPARTE
*Maxims*, 1804–15


When all is said and done, one loves one's country
not *because* of this or that, but rather, in spite of it
all.
ARTHUR KOESTLER, 1963


# Politics & Politicians

Politics is the art of the possible.
R. A. BUTLER


Political power grows out of the barrel of a gun.
MAO TSE-TUNG
*Quotations from Chairman Mao*, 1966


Moderation in the affairs of the nation is the
highest virtue.
LYNDON B. JOHNSON, 1964


You don't tell deliberate lies; but sometimes you
have to be evasive.
MARGARET THATCHER, 1976

You're not supposed to be so blind with patriotism
that you can't face reality. Wrong is wrong, no
matter who does it or who says it.

MALCOLM X<br>
*Malcolm X Speaks*, 1965

I should like to love my country and still love
justice.

ALBERT CAMUS<br>
*The Rebel*, 1951

# Politics & Politicians

Politics is not the art of the possible. It consists in
choosing between the disastrous and the
unpalatable.

J. K. GALBRAITH, 1969

The end move in politics is always to pick up a
gun.

R. BUCKMINSTER FULLER

I would remind you that extremism in the defense
of liberty is no vice. And let me remind you also
that moderation in the pursuit of justice is no
virtue.

BARRY GOLDWATER

Self-criticism is the secret weapon of democracy,
and candor and confession are good for the soul.

ADLAI STEVENSON, 1952

The sad duty of politics is to establish justice in a
sinful world.
REINHOLD NIEBUHR

If the Labour Party is anything, it is a moral
crusade.
HAROLD WILSON

All political parties die at last of swallowing their
own lies.
JOHN ARBUTHNOT

... to evolve policies from ideas, to organize mass
movements, to campaign for these policies, to
convince people to accept them, to carry through
the programme by consent, lubricating the process
with wise compromises without losing sight of the
objective as he goes along – these are the tasks of
the politician.
TONY BENN, 1964

We are not in politics to ignore people's worries;
we are in politics to deal with them.
MARGARET THATCHER

I was sent to this place to vote with my head, not
with my feet.
WINSTON CHURCHILL

The middle of the road is all of the usable surface.
The extremes, right and left, are in the gutters.
DWIGHT D. EISENHOWER

Your public servants serve you right; indeed often
they serve you better than your apathy and
indifference deserve.
ADLAI STEVENSON

Propaganda is that branch of the art of lying
which consists in nearly deceiving your friends
without quite deceiving your enemies.
F. M. CORNFORD, 1978

Doing what's right isn't the problem. It's knowing
what's right.

LYNDON B. JOHNSON

I have never regarded politics as the arena of
morals. It is the arena of interests.

ANEURIN BEVAN

The victor will never be asked if he told the truth.

ADOLF HITLER

... there is nobody in the world who submits to
anything but force.

ERNEST BEVIN

Many of our troubles are due to the fact that our
people turn to politicians for everything.

MARGARET THATCHER

I stand up when he nudges me. I sits down when
they pull my coat.

ERNEST BEVIN

We know what happens to people who stay in the
middle of the road. They get run over.

ANEURIN BEVAN

Politicians are the same all over. They promise to
build a bridge even when there's no river.

NIKITA KHRUSHCHEV

If you can't convince them, confuse them.

HARRY S. TRUMAN

The most successful politician is he who says what
everybody is thinking most often and in the
loudest voice.
THEODORE ROOSEVELT

Your representative owes you, not his industry
only, but his judgement; and he betrays instead of
serving you if he sacrifices it to your opinion.
EDMUND BURKE

Tyranny is the normal pattern of government. It is
only by intense thought, by great effort, by
burning idealism and unlimited sacrifice that
freedom has prevailed as a system of government.
ADLAI STEVENSON, 1952

The great enemy of truth is very often not the lie –
deliberate, contrived and dishonest – but the myth
– persistent, persuasive and unrealistic.
JOHN F. KENNEDY, 1962

# The Press

The press can only be a mirror – albeit a distorting
mirror ... – but it rarely lies because it dare not.
JAMES CAMERON, 1979

Accuracy to a newspaper is what virtue is to a
lady, but a newspaper can always print a
retraction.
ADLAI STEVENSON

A good newspaper ... is a nation talking to itself.
ARTHUR MILLER, 1961

It is a general popular error to imagine the loudest
complainers for the public to be the most anxious
for its welfare.

EDMUND BURKE

a politician is an arse upon / which everyone has
sat except a man.

E. E. CUMMINGS

There are two problems in my life. The political
ones are insoluble and the economic ones are
incomprehensible.

SIR ALEC DOUGLAS HOME

When a man speaks of the need for realism one
may be sure that this is always the prelude to some
bloody deed.

SIR ISAIAH BERLIN

# The Press

The man who never looks into a newspaper is
better informed than he who reads them;
inasmuch as he who knows nothing is nearer to
the truth than he whose mind is filled with
falsehood and errors.

THOMAS JEFFERSON, 1807

The broads who work in the press are the hookers
of the press. I might offer them a buck and a half.

FRANK SINATRA, 1974

As for modern journalism, it is not my business to
defend it. It justifies its own existence by the great
Darwinian principle of the survival of the
vulgarest.

OSCAR WILDE<br>Intentions, 1891

Ink-fresh papers, millions of them . . . How fine it is,
here in America, at ink-fresh, coffee-fragrant
morning, to read the paper.
THOMAS WOLFE
*You Can't Go Home Again,* 1940


Journalism is literature in a hurry.
MATTHEW ARNOLD


It is well to remember that freedom through the
press is the thing that comes first. Most of us
probably feel we couldn't be free without
newspapers . . .
ED MURROW

Like most censors he was perfectly convinced that
his own tastes were somehow in tune with the
music of the spheres . . . behind his complacency
lay the assumption of a Deity who had chosen to
infuse into the Best People a practically infallible
sense of what was right, what wrong.
E. M. HALLIDAY, on Dr Thomas Bowdler

Were it left to me to decide whether we should
have a government without newspapers, or
newspapers without a government, I should not
hesitate a moment to prefer the latter.
THOMAS JEFFERSON, 1787

The freedom of the press is one of the great
bulwarks of liberty, and can never be restrained
but by despotic government.
GEORGE MASON
*Virginia Bill of Rights,* 1776

The Press is easier squashed than squared.
WINSTON CHURCHILL

By and large the editors will have complete
freedom, as long as they agree with the policy I
have laid down.
LORD MATTHEWS, 1978

Every journal, from the first line to the last, is
nothing but a tissue of horrors . . . And it is with
this loathsome appetizer that civilized man daily
washes down his morning repast.

BAUDELAIRE<br>
Mon coeur mis à nu, 1887

Journalism is the ability to meet the challenge of
filling space.

DAME REBECCA WEST

If newspapers are useful in overthrowing tyrants,
it is only to establish a tyranny of their own.

JAMES FENIMORE COOPER

No member of a society has a right to teach any
doctrine contrary to what the society holds to be
true.

SAMUEL JOHNSON

Newspaper editors are men who separate the
wheat from the chaff, and then print the chaff.

ADLAI STEVENSON

No government ought to be without censors; and
where the press is free, no one ever will.

THOMAS JEFFERSON, 1792

Reporters are puppets. They simply respond to the
pull of the most powerful strings.

LYNDON B. JOHNSON

Everybody favors free speech in the slack moments
when no axes are being ground.

HEYWOOD BROUN

# Progress

The only limit to our realization of tomorrow will be our doubts of today.
FRANKLIN D. ROOSEVELT, 1945

Every advance in civilization has been denounced as unnatural while it was recent.
BERTRAND RUSSELL
*Unpopular Essays*, 1950

Progress is a comfortable disease.
E. E. CUMMINGS

Growth is the only evidence of life.
CARDINAL NEWMAN

The democratic philosophy of man and society has faith in the resources and the vocation of human nature.
JACQUES MARITAIN

Whatever there be of progress in life comes not through adaptation but through daring, through obeying the blind urge.
HENRY MILLER
*The Wisdom of the Heart*, 1941

The art of progress is to preserve order amid change and to preserve change amid order.
ALFRED NORTH WHITEHEAD

The desire to understand the world and the desire to reform it are the two great engines of progress, without which human society would stand still or retrogress.
BERTRAND RUSSELL

I doubt not through the ages one increasing purpose runs, / And the thoughts of men are widened with the process of the suns.
TENNYSON
"Locksley Hall", 1842

If you want a picture of the future, imagine a boot
stamping on the human face – forever . . .
GEORGE ORWELL, 1948

You can't say civilization don't advance, . . . for in
every war they kill you a new way.
WILL ROGERS
*The Autobiography of Will Rogers*, 1949

Every decision is like murder and our march
forward is over the stillborn bodies of all our
possible selves that will never be.
RENE DUBOIS

. . . growth is not only unneccessary, but ruinous.
ALEXANDER SOLZHENITSYN

. . . the ultimate direction of the common man's
democracy is in the direction of a police state –
burn the books; put the artist in prison; prevent
him telling the truth. The common man must be
flattered – not told the truth.
SIR OSBERT SITWELL

All progress means war with Society.
GEORGE BERNARD SHAW
*Getting Married*, 1911

Man's "progress" is but a gradual discovery that
his questions have no meaning.
SAINT-EXUPÉRY
*The Wisdom of the Sands*, 1948

Progress was all right. Only it went on too long.
JAMES THURBER (attrib.)

The simple faith in progress is not a conviction
belonging to strength, but one belonging to
acquiescence and hence to weakness.
NORBERT WIENER
*The Human Use of Human Beings*, 1954

All that is human must retrograde if it do not
advance.
EDWARD GIBBON
*Decline and Fall of the Roman Empire*, 1776

The reasonable man adapts himself to the world:
the unreasonable one persists in trying to adapt
the world to himself. Therefore all progress
depends on the unreasonable man.
GEORGE BERNARD SHAW
*Man and Superman*, 1903

Progress, man's distinctive mark alone, / Not
God's, and not the beasts': God is, they are; / Man
partly is, and wholly hopes to be.
ROBERT BROWNING
*Dramatis Personae*, 1864

# Psychiatry

Show me a sane man and I will cure him for you.
C. G. JUNG

Look into the depths of your own soul and learn
first to know yourself, then you will understand
why this illness was bound to come upon you and
perhaps you will thenceforth avoid falling ill.
SIGMUND FREUD
*Collected Papers*, 1924–50

Artists tend to be afraid of it. They think they'll lose
their creativity. But what analysis teaches you is
how to surrender yourself to your fantasies. How
to dive down into those fantasies.
ERICA JONG

Progress is man's ability to complicate simplicity.
<br>THOR HEYERDAHL
<br>*Fatu-hiva*, 1974

All progress is based upon a universal innate desire on the part of every organism to live beyond its income.
<br>SAMUEL BUTLER
<br>*Note-Books*, 1912

The fatal metaphor of progress, which means leaving things behind us, has utterly obscured the real idea of growth, which means leaving things inside us.
<br>G. K. CHESTERTON
<br>*Fancies Versus Fads*, 1923

# Psychiatry

I do not think our successes can compete with those of Lourdes.
<br>SIGMUND FREUD
<br>*Introductory Lectures*, 1917

All men should strive to learn before they die
<br>What they are running from, and to, and why.
<br>JAMES THURBER
<br>*Further Fables for Our Time*, 1956

Anybody who goes to see a psychiatrist ought to have his head examined.
<br>SAMUEL GOLDWYN (attrib.)

The unexamined life is not worth living.
SOCRATES
in Plato's *Apology*, 4th century B.C.


Know then thyself, presume not God to scan; / The
proper study of mankind is man.
POPE
*An Essay on Man*, 1733–4

It is far more important that one's life should be
perceived than that it should be transformed; for
no sooner has it been perceived, than it transforms
itself of its own accord.
MAURICE MAETERLINCK
*The Treasure of the Humble*, 1896

Let us not seek our disease outside ourselves; it is
in us, planted in our bowels, and the mere fact that
we do not perceive ourselves to be sick makes it
harder for us to be cured.
SENECA
*Letters to Lucilius*, 1st century A.D.

Whoever observes himself arrests his own
development. A caterpillar that wanted to know
itself well would never become a butterfly.
ANDRÉ GIDE
*Les Nouvelles Nourritures*, 1935

Self-knowledge is a dangerous thing, tending to
make man shallow or insane.
KARL SHAPIRO
*The Bourgeois Poet*, 1964

All the art of analysis consists in saying a truth
only when the other person is ready for it, has
been prepared for it by an organic process of
gradation and evolution.
ANAÏS NIN
*The Journals*

It seems a pity that psychology should have
destroyed our knowledge of human nature.
G. K. CHESTERTON, 1934

# Reason

We may take Fancy for a companion, but must
follow Reason as our guide.
SAMUEL JOHNSON


Logic is the art of making truth prevail.
LA BRUYÈRE


Reason alone is choice.
MILTON
*Paradise Lost,* 1667


The want of logic annoys ...
ANDRÉ GIDE
*Journals,* 1927


To a reasonable creature, that alone is
unsupportable which is unreasonable, but
everything reasonable may be supported.
EPICTETUS
*Discourses,* 1st century A.D.


Reason commands us far more imperiously than a
master; in disobeying the latter we are made
unhappy, in disobeying the former, fools.
PASCAL
*Pensées,* 1670


Reason means truth, and those who are not
governed by it take the chance that some day the
sunken fact will rip the bottom out of their boat.
OLIVER WENDELL HOLMES JR
*The Mind and Faith of Justice Holmes,* 1943

'tis the debt of our reason we owe unto God, and
the homage we pay for not being beasts.
SIR THOMAS BROWNE
*Religio Medici,* 1642

Reason? That dreary shed, that hutch for grubby schoolboys.

THEODORE ROETHKE
"I Cry, Love! Love!"

*Logic.* n. The art of thinking and reasoning in strict accordance with the limitations of the human misunderstanding.

AMBROSE BIERCE
*The Devil's Dictionary,* 1881–1911

Reason ruling alone is a force confining.

KAHLIL GIBRAN
*The Prophet,* 1926

Life eludes logic, and everything that logic alone constructs remains artificial and forced.

ANDRÉ GIDE
*Journals,* 1927

Man has such a prediliction for systems and abstract deductions that he … is ready to deny the evidence of his own senses only to justify his own logic.

DOSTOEVSKY
*Notes from Underground,* 1864

The man who listens to reason is lost: Reason enslaves all whose minds are not strong enough to master her.

GEORGE BERNARD SHAW
*Man & Superman,* 1903

I believe in instinct, not in reason. When reason is right, nine times out of ten it is impotent, and when it prevails, nine times out of ten it is wrong.

EDWARD MARSH

Reason is itself a matter of faith. It is an act of faith to assert that our thoughts have any relation to reality at all.

G. K. CHESTERTON
*Orthodoxy,* 1908

# Religion

God is the immemorial refuge of the incompetent, the helpless, the miserable. They find not only sanctuary in His arms, but also a kind of superiority, soothing to their macerated egos; He will set them above their betters.
H. L. MENCKEN
*Minority Report*, 1956

I can tell you that God is alive because I talked to him this morning.
BILLY GRAHAM, 1966

Faith may be defined briefly as an illogical belief in the occurrence of the improbable.
H. L. MENCKEN
*Prejudices, Third Series*, 1922

God is our refuge and strength, / A very present help in trouble.
Psalms 46:1

If your faith is opposed to experience, to human learning and investigation it is not worth the breath used in giving it expression.
EDGAR WATSON HOWE
*Ventures in Common Sense*, 1919

If we meet no gods, it is because we harbor none.
EMERSON
*The Conduct of Life*, 1860

Do we, holding that the gods exist, / deceive ourselves with unsubstantial dreams / and lies, while random careless chance and change / alone control the world?
EURIPIDES
*Hecuba*, c. 425 B.C.

No man observes the law of God but in applying his reason to it . . .
SARA COLERIDGE, 1825

God has not called me to be successful, He has
called me to be faithful.

MOTHER TERESA, 1980

If you talk to God you are praying; if God talks to
you, you have schizophrenia.

THOMAS SZASZ
*The Second Sin*, 1974

A God who let us prove his existence would be an
idol.

DIETRICH BONHOEFFER
*No Rusty Swords*, 1928

Lord forgive all the little tricks I play on you, and
I'll forgive the great big one you played on me.

ROBERT FROST (attrib.)

Faith is not a formula which is agreed to if the
weight of evidence favors it.

WALTER LIPPMANN
*A Preface to Morals*, 1929

*Faith.* n. Belief without evidence in what is told by
one who speaks without knowledge, of things
without parallel.

AMBROSE BIERCE
*The Devil's Dictionary*, 1881–1911

Console thyself, thou wouldst not seek Me, if thou
hadst not found Me.

PASCAL
*Pensées*, 1670

If the work of God could be comprehended by
reason, it would no longer be wonderful.

POPE GREGORY I

The glory of Christianity is to conquer by
forgiveness.
WILLIAM BLAKE
*Jerusalem*, 1804–20


Faith is to believe what you do not yet see, the
reward for this faith is to see what you believe.
ST AUGUSTINE
*Sermons*, 5th century


God is the beyond in the midst of our life.
DIETRICH BONHOEFFER


He that loveth not knoweth not God; for God is
love.
1 John 4:8


An atheist is a man who has no invisible means of
support.
JOHN BUCHAN


The English Bible – a book which if everything else
in our language should perish would alone suffice
to show the whole extent of its beauty and power.
MACAULAY
"On John Dryden", 1828


I have found in it words for my inmost thoughts,
songs for my joy, utterance for my hidden griefs,
and pleadings for my shame and feebleness.
COLERIDGE


O Almighty God, who has knit together thine
elect . . . Grant us grace so to follow thy blessed
saints . . .
*Book of Common Prayer*, 1662


The three great elements of modern civilization,
Gunpowder, Printing, and the Protestant Religion.
THOMAS CARLYLE

Christians have burnt each other, quite
persuaded / That all the Apostles would have done
as they did.

BYRON
*Don Juan*, 1819–24

Faith is, before all and above all, wishing God may
exist.

MIGUEL DE UNAMUNO
*Tragic Sense of Life*, 1913

If only God would give me a clear sign! Like
making a large deposit in my name at a Swiss
bank.

WOODY ALLEN

God is love, but get it in writing.

GYPSY ROSE LEE (attrib.)

I am an atheist still, thank God.

LUIS BUÑUEL

Those who talk of the Bible as a "monument of
English prose" are merely admiring it as a
monument over the grave of Christianity.

T. S. ELIOT
"Religion and Literature", 1935

It (the Bible) is a history of wickedness that has
served to corrupt and brutalize mankind.

THOMAS PAINE

Martyrdom is the only way in which a man can
become famous without ability.

GEORGE BERNARD SHAW
*Essays in Fabian Socialism*, 1932

The chief contribution of Protestantism to human
thought is its massive proof that God is a bore.

H. L. MENCKEN

Clergy are men as well as other folks.
HENRY FIELDING
*Joseph Andrews*, 1742

It is clearly absurd that it should be possible for a
woman to qualify as a saint with direct access to
the Almighty while she may not qualify as a
curate.
MARY STOCKS

# Revolution

This country, with its institutions, belongs to the
people who inhabit it. Whenever they shall grow
weary of the existing Government, they can
exercise their constitutional right of amending it,
or their revolutionary right to dismember or
overthrow it.
ABRAHAM LINCOLN

There can never be an excuse for public disorder or
rioting.
WILLIAM WHITELAW, 1983

When I refuse to obey an unjust law, I do not
contest the right of the majority to command, but I
simply appeal from the sovereignty of the people to
the sovereignty of mankind.
DE TOCQUEVILLE
*Democracy in America*, 1835–9

As the French say, there are three sexes – men,
women, and clergymen.

SYDNEY SMITH

The souls of women are so small, / That some
believe they've none at all.

SAMUEL BUTLER<br>"Miscellaneous Thoughts"

# Revolution

To despise legitimate authority, no matter in what
it is invested, is unlawful; it is rebellion against
God's will.

POPE LEO XIII

If the State acts in ways abhorrent to human
nature, it is the lesser evil to destroy it.

SPINOZA

Disobedience is the worst of evils. This it is what
ruins a nation.

JEAN ANOUILH

Let me say ... that the true revolutionary is guided
by a great feeling of love.
CHE GUEVARA


The moment you have a plan you cease to be a
revolutionary.
DANIEL COHN-BENDIT, 1968


Terrorism is essentially the rage of literati in its last
stage.
JACOB BURCKHARDT


The tree of liberty must be refreshed from time to
time with the blood of patriots and tyrants. It is its
natural manure.
THOMAS JEFFERSON, 1787


Revolution ... cannot be advanced softly,
gradually, carefully, considerately, respectfully,
politely, plainly and modestly.
MAO TSE-TUNG


We live in a hemisphere whose own revolution has
given birth to the most powerful force of the
modern age – the search for the freedom and self-
fulfillment of man.
JOHN F. KENNEDY, 1961


A little rebellion, now and then, is a good thing,
and as necessary in the political world as storms in
the physical.
THOMAS JEFFERSON, 1787


A great revolution is never the fault of the people,
but of the government.
GOETHE
in Eckermann, *Conversations with Goethe*, 1847

In revolutions authority remains with the greatest
scoundrels.
DANTON, 1759–94

The moment you *cease* to have a plan, you cease to
be a revolution – you are a rabble.
KENNETH TYNAN

Revolutions are not made with literature.
Revolutions equal gunfire.
FRANÇOIS DUVALIER, 1964

Every revolution evaporates, leaving behind only
the slime of a new bureaucracy.
FRANZ KAFKA (attrib.)

Revolutions have never succeeded unless the
establishment does three-quarters of the work.
PETER USTINOV<br>*Dear Me*, 1977

Great cultural changes begin in affectation and
end in routine.
JACQUES BARZUN<br>*The House of Intellect*, 1959

The world is always childish, and with each new
gewgaw of a revolution or new constitution that it
finds, thinks it shall never cry any more.
EMERSON<br>*Journals*, 1847

The overwhelming pressure of mediocrity,
sluggish and indomitable as a glacier, will mitigate
the most violent, and depress the most exalted
revolution.
T. S. ELIOT<br>"The Idea of a Christian Society", 1939

If the abuse be enormous, nature will rise up, and
claiming her original rights, overturn a corrupt
political system.
SAMUEL JOHNSON
In Boswell, *Life of Johnson*, 1791

All oppressed people are authorized, whenever
they can, to rise and break their fetters.
HENRY CLAY, 1818


Most revolutionaries are potential Tories, because
they imagine that everything can be put right by
altering the shape of society; once that change is
effected – as it sometimes is – they see no need for
any other.
GEORGE ORWELL
*Inside the Whale*, 1950

Those who make peaceful revolution impossible
will make violent revolution inevitable.
JOHN F. KENNEDY

Revolutions are not made by fate but by men.
JACOB BRONOWSKI<br>*The Ascent of Man*, 1973

All modern revolutions have ended in a
reinforcement of the power of the State.
ALBERT CAMUS<br>*The Rebel*, 1951

The successful revolutionary is a statesman, the
unsuccessful one a criminal.
ERICH FROMM<br>*Escape from Freedom*, 1941

Revolutions have never lightened the burden of
tyranny: they have only shifted it to another
shoulder.
GEORGE BERNARD SHAW<br>*Man and Superman*, 1903

# Risk & Caution

Audacity augments courage; hesitation, fear.
PUBLILIUS SYRUS
*Moral Sayings*, 1st century B.C.


Unless you enter the tiger's den you cannot take
the cubs.
Japanese proverb


Delay always breeds danger . . .
CERVANTES
*Don Quixote*, 1605–15


With audacity one can undertake anything.
NAPOLEON BONAPARTE
*Maxims*, 1804–15


Yield not thy neck / To fortune's yoke, but let thy
dauntless mind / Still ride in triumph over all
mischance.
SHAKESPEARE
*3 Henry VI*, 1592


If the creator had a purpose in equipping us with a
neck, he surely meant us to stick it out.
ARTHUR KOESTLER, 1970


The torment of precautions often exceeds the
dangers to be avoided. It is sometimes better to
abandon one's self to destiny.
NAPOLEON BONAPARTE
*Maxims*, 1804–15


Life is either a daring adventure or nothing.
HELEN KELLER
*Let Us Have Faith*, 1940


Oh isn't life a terrible thing, thank God?
DYLAN THOMAS
*Under Milk Wood*

# Risk & Caution

It is well to moor your ship with two anchors.
PUBLILIUS SYRUS
*Moral Sayings*, 1st century B.C.

He who wants a rose must respect a thorn.
Persian proverb

Delay is preferable to error.
THOMAS JEFFERSON, 1792

If thy heart fails thee, climb not at all.
THOMAS FULLER
*Worthies of England*, 1662

The better part of valour is discretion.
SHAKESPEARE
*1 Henry IV*, 1597

Never be a pioneer. It's the Early Christian that
gets the fattest lion.
SAKI (H. H. MUNRO)
*Reginald*, 1904

To hazard much to get much has more of avarice
than wisdom.
WILLIAM PENN
*Some Fruits of Solitude*, 1693

... a life in which adventure is allowed to take
whatever form it will is sure to be short.
BERTRAND RUSSELL
*Authority and the Individual*, 1949

Life is a gamble, at terrible odds – if it was a bet,
you wouldn't take it.
TOM STOPPARD
*Rosencrantz and Guildenstern are Dead*, 1967

# Science

Science, by itself, cannot supply us with an ethic.
BERTRAND RUSSELL, 1950


The true men of action in our time, those who
transform the world, are not the politicians and
statesmen, but the scientists.
W. H. AUDEN
*The Dyer's Art*, 1963


When I find myself in the company of scientists, I
feel like a shabby curate who has strayed by
mistake into a drawing-room full of dukes.
W. H. AUDEN
*The Dyer's Art*, 1963

If a man's wit be wandering, let him study the
mathematics.
FRANCIS BACON
*Essays*, 1625

The true spirit of delight, the exaltation, the sense
of being more than Man, which is the touchstone
of the highest excellence, is to be found in
mathematics as surely as in poetry.
BERTRAND RUSSELL
*Mysticism and Logic*, 1917

The secret of science is to ask the right question,
and it is the choice of problem more than anything
else that marks the man of genius in the scientific
world.
SIR HENRY TIZARD

Science knows only one commandment:
contribute to science.
BERTOLT BRECHT
*Galileo*, 1943

Science is nothing but trained and organized
common sense.
T. H. HUXLEY

# Science

Our scientific power has outrun our spiritual
power. We have guided missiles and misguided
men.

MARTIN LUTHER KING JR<br>
*Strength to Love*, 1963

We have genuflected before the god of science only
to find that it has given us the atomic bomb,
producing fears and anxieties that science can
never mitigate.

MARTIN LUTHER KING JR<br>
*Strength to Love*, 1963

There are no great men save the poet, the priest
and the soldier. The man who sings, the man who
offers up sacrifice, and the man who sacrifices
himself. The rest are born for the whip.

BAUDELAIRE

I don't believe in mathematics.

ALBERT EINSTEIN

Mathematics is the only science where one never
knows what one is talking about nor whether
what is said is true.

BERTRAND RUSSELL<br>
*Mysticism and Logic*, 1917

I have yet to see any problem, however
complicated, which, when you looked at it in the
right way, did not become more complicated.

POUL ANDERSON, 1969

The discovery of a new dish does more for the
happiness of mankind than the discovery of a star.

BRILLAT-SAVARIN<br>
*The Physiology of Taste*, 1825

As far as the laws of mathematics refer to reality,
they are not certain, and as far as they are certain,
they do not refer to reality.

ALBERT EINSTEIN

# Sex

Sex is one of the nine reasons for re-incarnation.
. . . The other eight are unimportant.
HENRY MILLER
*Big Sur and the Oranges of Hieronymous Bosch,*
1957


The zipless fuck is absolutely pure . . . and it is rarer
than the unicorn.
ERICA JONG
*Fear of Flying,* 1973


A bird in the hand is worth two in the bush.
traditional


Make us, not fly to dreams, but moderate desire.
MATTHEW ARNOLD
*Empedocles on Etna,* 1852


Let's do it; let's fall in love.
COLE PORTER
"Let's Do It"


I still have a diary entry . . . asking myself whether
talk about the size of the male organ isn't a
homosexual preoccupation: if things aren't too
bad in other ways I doubt if any woman cares
much.
LILLIAN HELLMAN
*Pentimento,* 1973


Familiar acts are beautiful through love.
SHELLEY
*Prometheus Unbound,* 1818–19


Sex, treated properly can be one of the most
gorgeous things in the world.
ELIZABETH TAYLOR, 1969

All this fuss about sleeping together. For physical pleasure I'd sooner go to my dentist any day.

EVELYN WAUGH
*Vile Bodies*, 1930

It is all this cold-hearted fucking that is death and idiocy.

D. H. LAWRENCE
*Lady Chatterley's Lover*, 1928

One in the bush is worth two in the hand.

graffito

Our desires, once realized, haunt us again less readily.

MARGARET FULLER
*Summer on the Lakes*, 1844

It's not 'cause I wouldn't / It's not 'cause I shouldn't / And, Lord knows, it's not 'cause I couldn't, / It's simply because I'm the laziest girl in town.

COLE PORTER
"The Laziest Girl in Town"

Only good girls keep diaries. Bad girls don't have the time.

TALLULAH BANKHEAD (attrib.)

Familiarity breeds contempt – and children.

MARK TWAIN
*Notebook*, 1935

People kill each other in bed. Some of the greatest crimes ever committed were committed in bed. And no weapons were used.

NORMAN MAILER, 1968

I've tried several varieties of sex. The conventional
position makes me claustrophobic. And the others
either give me a stiff neck or lockjaw.
TALLULAH BANKHEAD (attrib.)

All God's Chillun Got Rhythm.
GUS KAHN, song title


If you cannot be chaste, be cautious.
Spanish proverb


Candy / Is dandy / But liquor / Is quicker.
OGDEN NASH
*Verses from 1929 On*, 1959


"Bed", as the Italian proverb succinctly puts it, "is
the poor man's opera."
ALDOUS HUXLEY
*Heaven and Hell*, 1956

The two best subjects for conversation are talking
shop and making love.
PHYLLIS BOTTOME
*Ladies' Home Journal*


Love is the answer, but while you are waiting for
the answer, sex raises some pretty good questions.
WOODY ALLEN, 1975

I have married a wife, and therefore I cannot
come.

Luke 14:20

Yes sir. That's my baby, / No sir, don't mean
maybe; / Yes sir, that's my baby now.

GUS KAHN<br>"Yes Sir, That's My Baby"

Chastity – the most unnatural of the sexual
perversions.

ALDOUS HUXLEY

Sex is only the liquid centre of the great Newberry
Fruit of friendship.

JILLY COOPER<br>Super-Jilly, 1977

Anyone who says he can see through women is
missing a lot.

GROUCHO MARX

Sex as an institution, sex as a general notion, sex
as a problem, sex as a platitude – all this is
something I find too tedious for words. Let us skip
sex.

VLADIMIR NABOKOV<br>Strong Opinions, 1973

The pleasure is momentary, the position
ridiculous, and the expense damnable.

LORD CHESTERFIELD

Communism deprives no man of the power to appropriate the products of society; all it does is to deprive him of the power to subjugate the labour of others by means of such appropriation.
MARX AND ENGELS
*The Communist Manifesto*, 1848


The language of priorities is the religion of socialism.
ANEURIN BEVAN


Communists have committed great crimes, but at least they have not stood aside. . . . I would rather have blood on my hands than water, like Pilate.
GRAHAM GREENE
*The Comedians*, 1966


The substitution of the proletarian for the bourgeois state is impossible without a violent revolution.
LENIN
*State and Revolution*, 1917


I have seen the future and it works.
LINCOLN STEFFENS, returning from the USSR, 1919


My idea of a Labour Government is one which fulfils its election pledges to build a new Jerusalem, which is not a corny ideal.
ERIC HEFFER, 1975


Communism is a society where each one works according to his ability and gets according to his needs.
PROUDHON


The theory of communism may be summed up in one sentence: Abolition of private property.
MARX AND ENGELS
*The Communist Manifesto*, 1848

What is a communist? One who has yearnings /
For equal division of unequal earnings.

EBENEZER ELLIOTT
*Poetical Works*, 1840

As with the Christian religion, the worst
advertisement for Socialism is its adherents.

GEORGE ORWELL
*The Road to Wigan Pier*, 1937

The function of socialism is to raise suffering to a
higher level.

NORMAN MAILER

Socialism can only arrive by bicycle.

JOSÉ ANTONIO VIERA GALLO

For us in Russia, communism is a dead dog, while
for many people in the West, it is still a living lion.

ALEXANDER SOLZHENITSYN, 1979

Heaven on earth is not tomorrow.

JAMES CALLAGHAN, 1979

Communism is the corruption of a dream of
justice.

ADLAI STEVENSON, 1951

Socialism is nothing but the capitalism of the lower
classes.

OSWALD SPENGLER

# Sport

Sport is an order of chivalry, a code of ethics and
aesthetics, recruiting its members from all classes
and all peoples. Sport is a truce . . .
RENE MAHEU

There is something noble in defeat. You cannot
find victory unless you first understand defeat.
DUANE THOMAS, after a Super Bowl defeat, 1971

By the way, what a polite game tennis is. The chief
word seems to be "sorry" and admiration of each
other's play crosses the net as frequently as the
ball.
J. M. BARRIE

Chess is like playing at a concert. That's where it's
at. Some day I'm going to dress for a show, I mean
a game, like Tom Jones or Liberace.
BOBBY FISCHER, 1972

Nobody gets hurt but the customer.
JOE LOUIS

Golf is like a love affair: if you don't take it
seriously, it's no fun; if you do take it seriously, it
breaks your heart.
ARNOLD DALY

What is human life but a game of cricket?
DUKE OF DORSET, 1777

Serious sport has nothing to do with fair play. It is bound up with hatred, jealousy, boastfulness, disregard of all rules and sadistic pleasure in witnessing violence: in other words it is war minus the shooting.

GEORGE ORWELL
"The Sporting Spirit", 1945


Do you know what happens after you lose the Super Bowl? The world ends. It just stops.

JOE KAPP, after a Super Bowl defeat, 1970


How wonderful it is to look over after smashing the ball he cannot see and watch how he cannot move and see him split in half.

ILIE NASTASE, 1972


It is a game too troublesome for some men's brains, too testy full of anxiety, all out as bad as study; besides it is a cholericke game, and very offensive to him who lose the Mate.

BURTON, on chess
*The Anatomy of Melancholy*, 1621


It's like someone jammed an electric light bulb in your face and busted it. I thought half my head was blowed off.

JIM BRADDOCK, on being hit by Joe Louis


Golf is a good walk spoiled.

MARK TWAIN


Personally, I have always looked upon cricket as organized loafing.

WILLIAM TEMPLE
Archbishop of Canterbury, 1925

# Success

Doing is overrated, and success undesirable, but
the bitterness of failure even more so.
CYRIL CONNOLLY
*The Unquiet Grave*, 1944

Success and failure are both difficult to endure.
Along with success come drugs, divorce,
fornication, bullying, travel, meditation,
medication, depression, neurosis and suicide. With
failure comes failure.
JOSEPH HELLER, 1975

. . . the world can only be grasped by action, not by
contemplation. The hand is more important than
the eye . . . The hand is the cutting edge of the
mind.
JACOB BRONOWSKI
*The Ascent of Man*, 1973

The common idea that success spoils people by
making them vain, egotistic, and self complacent is
erroneous – on the contrary it makes them, for the
most part, humble, tolerant and kind, Failure
makes people bitter and cruel.
W. SOMERSET MAUGHAM

He that riseth late must trot all day.
BENJAMIN FRANKLIN
*Poor Richard's Almanack*, 1732–57

Few things are impossible to diligence and skill.
SAMUEL JOHNSON
*Rasselas*, 1759

Those whom the Gods wish to destroy they first
call promising.
CYRIL CONNOLLY, 1977

Care and diligence bring luck.
THOMAS FULLER
*Gnomologia*, 1732

Failure is lovable and what is lovable is commercial.

> V. S. PRITCHETT
> *The Living Novel and the Later Appreciations*, 1964

There is much to be said for failure. It is more interesting than success.

> MAX BEERBOHM
> *Mainly On the Air*, 1946

We must believe in luck. For how else can we explain the success of those we don't like?

> JEAN COCTEAU

Winners got scars too.

> JOHNNY CASH

Early to bed, early to rise, makes a man healthy, wealthy and dead.

> JAMES THURBER
> *Fables for Our Time*, 1951

You can't make the Duchess of Windsor into Rebecca of Sunnybrook Farm. The facts of life are very stubborn things.

> CLEVELAND AMORY, 1955

Whom the mad would destroy they first make Gods.

> BERNARD LEVIN, 1967

Of course there is no formula for success, except perhaps, an unconditional acceptance of life and what it brings.

> ARTHUR RUBINSTEIN, 1974

For most people the fantasy is driving around in a
big car, having all the chicks you want and being
able to pay for it. It always has been, still is, and
always will be. Anyone who says it isn't is talking
bullshit.
MICK JAGGER

If you aspire to the highest place, it is no disgrace
to stop at the second, or even the third, place.
CICERO
*On Oratory*, 55 B.C.

Who is content with nothing possesses all things.
BOILEAU
*Epîtres*, 1669

The greatest humiliation in life is to work hard on
something from which you expect great
appreciation, and then fail to get it.
EDGAR WATSON HOWE
*Ventures in Common Sense*, 1919

What I must do is all that concerns me. Not what
the people think.
EMERSON
*Essays, First Series*, 1841

A man's worth is no greater than the worth of his
ambitions.
MARCUS AURELIUS
*Meditations*, 2nd century A.D.

To have a grievance is to have a purpose in life.
ERIC HOFFER
*The Passionate State of Mind,* 1954


Nothing is surely a waste of time when one enjoys
the day.
ARTHUR KOESTLER


Blessed is he who expects nothing, for he shall
never be disappointed.
POPE, 1727

There are only the pursued, the pursuing, the
busy, and the tired.
F. SCOTT FITZGERALD
*The Great Gatsby,* 1926


The men who really believe in themselves are all in
lunatic asylums.
G. K. CHESTERTON
*Orthodoxy,* 1908

Ambition makes more trusty slaves than need.
BEN JONSON
*Sejanus,* 1603

Travel ⟩

A man of ordinary talent will always be ordinary, whether he travels or not; but a man of superior talent (which I cannot deny myself to be without being impious) will go to pieces if he remains forever in the same place . . .
MOZART, 1778

For my part, I travel not to go anywhere, but to go. I travel for travel's sake. The great affair is to move.
ROBERT LOUIS STEVENSON
*Travels with a Donkey*, 1879

Being in a ship is being in a jail, with the chance of being drowned.
SAMUEL JOHNSON
in Boswell, *Life of Johnson*, 1791

The great and recurrent question about abroad is, is it worth getting there?
ROSE MACAULAY (attrib.)

Many shall run to and fro, and knowledge shall be increased.
Daniel 12:4

I travelled among unknown men, / In lands beyond the sea; / Nor, England! did I know till then / What love I bore to thee.
WORDSWORTH
"I Travelled Among Unknown Men", 1801

They [railway termini] are our gates to the glorious and the unknown. Through them we pass out into adventure and sunshine, and to them, alas! we return.
E. M. FORSTER
*Howards End*, 1910

But why, oh why, do the wrong people travel, /
When the right people stay at home?

NOËL COWARD
*Sail Away*

What gives value to travel is fear .... There is no
pleasure in travelling, and I look upon it more as
an occasion for spiritual testing.

ALBERT CAMUS
*Notebooks*, 1962

Lovers of air travel find it exhilarating to hang
poised between the illusion of immortality and the
fact of death.

ALEXANDER CHASE
*Perspectives*, 1966

All places are distant from heaven alike.

BURTON
*Anatomy of Melancholy*, 1621

In travelling: a man must carry knowledge with
him, if he would bring home knowledge.

SAMUEL JOHNSON
in Boswell, *Life of Johnson*, 1791

When one realizes that his life is worthless he
either commits suicide or travels.

EDWARD DAHLBERG
*Reasons of the Heart*, 1965

Whenever I prepare for a journey I prepare as
though for death.

KATHERINE MANSFIELD
*Journal*, 1922

Everything in life is somewhere else . . .
E. B. WHITE

It is suicide to be abroad. But what is it to be at
home? A lingering dissolution.
SAMUEL BECKETT

He that travels much knows much.
THOMAS FULLER
*Gnomologia*, 1732

The choice and nature of our holidays is more than
anything in our lives an expression of ourselves.
ALEC WAUGH

Travelling. This makes men wiser, but less happy.
THOMAS JEFFERSON, 1787

All of us, from time to time, need a plunge into
freedom and novelty, after which routine and
discipline will seem delightful by contrast.
ANDRÉ MAUROIS
*The Art of Living*, 1940

Afoot and light-hearted I take to the open road, /
Healthy, free, the world before me . . .
WALT WHITMAN
"Song of the Open Road", 1855

It is not irritating to be where one is. It is only
irritating to think one would like to be somewhere
else.

JOHN CAGE<br>
Silence, 1961

Abroad is bloody.

KING GEORGE VI (attrib.)

How much a dunce that has been sent to roam /
Excels a dunce that has been kept at home!

WILLIAM COWPER<br>
"The Progress of Error", 1782

... most men lead flat and virtuous lives, departing
annually with their family to some flat and
virtuous place, there to disport themselves in a
manner that is decent, orderly, wholly
uninteresting, vacant of every buxom stimulus. To
such as these a suggestion ... why not try crime?

KENNETH GRAHAME

Travelling is a fool's paradise. We owe to our first
journeys the discovery that place is nothing.

EMERSON<br>
Essays: First Series, 1841

Holidays are often overrated disturbances of
routine, costly and uncomfortable, and they
usually need another holiday to correct their
ravages.

E. V. LUCAS

Road. n. A strip of land along which one may pass
from where it is too tiresome to be to where it is
futile to go.

AMBROSE BIERCE<br>
The Devil's Dictionary, 1881–1911

# War

Battle is the most magnificent competition in which a human being can indulge. It brings out all that is best; it removes all that is base.
GENERAL GEORGE S. PATTON

War can only be abolished through war, and in order to get rid of the gun it is necessary to take up the gun.
MAO TSE-TUNG
*Quotations from Chairman Mao*, 1966

Life and fame and wealth – all these must, I say, be defended by fighting. Death in battle is the most glorious for men. Who lives under the sway of his foe – it is he that is dead.
*Panchatantra, c.* 5th century B.C.

War makes strange giant creatures out of us little routine men who inhabit the earth.
ERNIE PYLE

Total victory in Vietnam means peace.
CARDINAL SPELLMAN, 1967

To fight is a radical instinct; if men have nothing else to fight over they will fight over words, fancies, or women, or they will fight because they dislike each other's looks, or because they have met walking in opposite directions.
GEORGE SANTAYANA
*The Life of Reason*, 1905–6

War may make a fool of man, but it by no means degrades him; on the contrary, it tends to exalt him, and its net effects are much like those of motherhood on women.
H. L. MENCKEN
*Minority Report*, 1956

If we lose this war, I'll start another in my wife's name.
MOSHE DAYAN

# War

To the ashes of the dead glory comes too late.

MARTIAL
*Epigrams*, A.D. 86


Everything that steel achieves in war can be won
in politics by eloquence.

DEMETRIUS
4th–3rd centuries B.C.


Dead men have no victory.

EURIPIDES
*The Phoenician Women*, 411–409 B.C.


I have never understood this liking for war. It
panders to instincts already catered for within the
scope of any respectable domestic establishment.

ALAN BENNETT
*40 Years On*, 1969

Peace is a continuation of war by other means.

GENERAL GIAP, 1973

There has never been a war yet which, if the facts
had been put calmly before the ordinary folk, could
not have been prevented. The common man is the
greatest protection against war.

ERNEST BEVIN, 1945


I do like to see the arms and legs fly.

COLONEL GEORGE S. PATTON


Sometime they will give a war and nobody will
come.

CARL SANDBURG
"The People, Yes", 1936

Human war has been the most successful of our
cultural traditions.
ROBERT ARDREY

We are going to have peace even if we have to fight
for it.
DWIGHT D. EISENHOWER

Ah God, how pretty war is, with its songs, its long
rests!
GUILLAUME APOLLINAIRE
"L'Adieu de Cavalier"

Everlasting peace is a dream, and not even a
pleasant one; and war is a necessary part of God's
arrangement of the world . . .
VON MOLTKE, 1880

There is hardly such a thing as a war in which it
makes no difference who wins. Nearly always one
side stands more or less for progress, the other side
more or less for reaction.
GEORGE ORWELL

All the poet can do today is warn. / That is why the
true Poets must be truthful.
WILFRED OWEN
"Anthem for Doomed Youth", *Poems*, 1920

I love war and responsibility and excitement.
Peace is going to be hell on me.
GENERAL GEORGE S. PATTON

War is the trade of kings.
DRYDEN
*King Arthur*, 1695

Either war is obsolete, or men are.

R. BUCKMINSTER FULLER, 1966

What difference does it make to the dead, the orphans and the homeless, whether the mad destruction is wrought under the name of totalitarianism or the holy name of liberty and democracy?

M. K. GANDHI<br>
*Non-Violence in Peace and War*, 1948

One of the essential experiences of war is never being able to escape from disgusting smells of human origin.

GEORGE ORWELL<br>
"Looking Back on the Spanish War", 1943

There never was a good war, or a bad peace.

BENJAMIN FRANKLIN, 1789

In war, whichever side may call itself the victor, there are no winners, but all are losers.

NEVILLE CHAMBERLAIN, 1938

The first casualty when war comes is truth.

PHILLIP KNIGHTLEY<br>
*The First Casualty*, 1975

One to destroy is murder by the law; / and gibbets keep the lifted hand in awe; / To murder thousands takes a specious name, / War's glorious art, and gives immortal fame.

EDWARD YOUNG<br>
"Love of Fame", 1725–8

But war's a game, which, were their subjects wise, Kings would not play at.

WILLIAM COWPER<br>
*The Task*, 1785

# Wealth

When I was young I thought money was the most important thing in life; now that I am old I know that it is.
OSCAR WILDE

A man who has a million dollars is as well off as if he were rich.
JOHN JACOB ASTOR III

A borrowed cloak does not keep one warm.
Arabic proverb

We are not concerned with the very poor. They are unthinkable, and only to be approached by the statistician or the poet.
E. M. FORSTER
*Howard's End*, 1910

I would rather be able to appreciate things I can not have than to have things I am not able to appreciate.
ELBURT HUBBARD
*The Note Book*, 1927

Undeserving poverty is my line. Taking one station with another, it's – it's – well, it's the only one that has any ginger in it, to my taste.
GEORGE BERNARD SHAW
*Pygmalion*, 1912

There are but two ways of paying debt: increase of industry in raising income, increase of thrift in laying out.
THOMAS CARLYLE
*Past and Present*, 1843

If a little does not go out, much cash will not come in.
Chinese proverb

Making money ain't nothing exciting to me. You might be able to buy a little better booze than the wino on the corner. But you get sick just like the next cat and when you die you're just as graveyard dead.

LOUIS ARMSTRONG, 1970

If you can count your money then you are not a really rich man.

PAUL GETTY

To be successful, keep looking tanned, live in an elegant building (even if you're in the cellar), be seen in smart restaurants (even if you nurse one drink) and if you borrow, borrow big.

ARISTOTLE ONASSIS, 1972

The poor man commands respect . . .

NAPOLEON BONAPARTE<br>Maxims, 1804–15

Hay is more acceptable to an ass than gold.

Latin proverb

Money is better than poverty, if only for financial reasons.

WOODY ALLEN<br>Without Feathers, 1972

Say nothing of my debts unless you mean to pay them.

English proverb

I don't commit any capital, I just make it.

ALBERT 'CUBBY' BROCCOLI, 1979

Let a man start out in life to build something better
and sell it cheaper than it has been built or sold
before, let him have that determination and the
money will roll in.
HENRY FORD I

Let the fruition of things bless the possession of
them, and take no satisfaction in dying but living
rich.
SIR THOMAS BROWNE

Listen sonny, when you're as wealthy as I am, you
can be what you damn well want.
PABLO PICASSO

Neither a borrower nor a lender be; / For loan oft
loses both itself and friend.
SHAKESPEARE
*Hamlet*, 1603

Philanthropy is commendable, but it must not
cause the philanthropist to overlook the
circumstances of economic injustice which make
philanthropy necessary.
MARTIN LUTHER KING JR

It is difficult but not impossible to conduct strictly
honest business. What is true is that honesty is
incompatible with the amassing of a large fortune.
M. K. GANDHI
*Non-Violence in Peace and War*, 1948

No one would remember the Good Samaritan if he
only had good intentions. He had money as well.
MARGARET THATCHER, 1980

If all the rich men in the world divided up their
money amongst themselves, there wouldn't be
enough to go round.
CHRISTINA STEAD
*House of All Nations*, 1938

The rich are different from us.
F. SCOTT FITZGERALD

Wealth is not the fruit of labour but the result of
organized, protected robbery.

FRANTZ FANON

There is a great deal of truth in Andrew Carnegie's
remark "The man who dies rich dies disgraced." I
should add, the man who lives rich, lives
disgraced.

AGA KHAN III

Money is like manure. You have to spread it
around or it smells.

J. PAUL GETTY

So soon as prudence has begun to grow up in the
brain, like a dismal fungus, it finds its own
expression in a paralysis of generous acts.

ROBERT LOUIS STEVENSON

Nothing links man to man like the frequent
passage from hand to hand of cash.

WALTER SICKERT

The fact that a business is large, efficient and
profitable does not mean it takes advantage of the
public.

CHARLES CLORE, 1974

The only thing I like about rich people is their
money.

NANCY ASTOR

The average man is rich enough when he has a
little more than he has got, and not till then.

DEAN INGE<br>
Outspoken Essays, First Series, 1919

Yes, they have more money.

ERNEST HEMINGWAY,<br>
replying to Scott Fitzgerald

# Wickedness

When you choose the lesser of two evils, always remember that it is still an evil.
MAX LERNER
*Actions and Passions*, 1949

As iron is eaten away by rust, so the envious are consumed by their own passion.
ANTISTHENES
5th–4th centuries B.C.

All sins tend to be addictive, and the terminal point of addiction is what is called damnation.
W. H. AUDEN
*A Certain World*, 1971

I detest that man, who / hides one thing in the depth of his heart, and speaks forth another.
HOMER
*Iliad*, 9th century B.C.

. . . the lie shall rot; / The truth is great, and shall prevail.
COVENTRY PATMORE
*The Unknown Eros*, 1877–90

The wickedness of the world is so great you have to run your legs off to avoid having them stolen from under you.
BERTOLT BRECHT
*The Threepenny Opera*, 1928

Men have never been good, they are not good, they never will be good.
KARL BARTH, 1954

Good can imagine Evil, but Evil cannot imagine Good.
W. H. AUDEN
*A Certain World*, 1971

Father I cannot tell a lie. I did it with my little hatchet.
GEORGE WASHINGTON

# Wickedness

Between two evils, I always pick the one I never tried before.

MAE WEST
in *Klondike Annie*, 1936

He who goes unenvied shall not be admired.

AESCHYLUS
*Agamemnon*, 458 B.C.

What after all / Is a halo? It's only one more thing to keep clean.

CHRISTOPHER FRY
*The Lady's Not for Burning*, 1949

Hypocrisy is the homage which vice pays to virtue.

LA ROCHEFOUCAULD
*Maxims*, 1665

A lie is an abomination unto the Lord and a very present help in trouble.

ADLAI STEVENSON, 1951

There is nothing either good or bad but thinking makes it so.

SHAKESPEARE
*Hamlet*, 1600

It is absurd to divide people into good and bad. People are either charming or tedious.

OSCAR WILDE
*The Portrait of Mr. W. H.*, 1901

Vice is its own reward.

QUENTIN CRISP
*The Naked Civil Servant*, 1968

Any fool can tell the truth, but it requires a man of some sense to know how to tell a lie well.

SAMUEL BUTLER
*Note-Books*, 1912

Anger would inflict punishment on another;
meanwhile it tortures itself.
PUBLILIUS SYRUS
*Moral Sayings*, 1st century B.C.


Angry men are blind and foolish . . .
PIETRO ARETINO, 1537


# Work >

Work is much more fun than fun.
NOËL COWARD, 1963


If a man does not work passionately (even
furiously) at being the best in the world at what he
does, he fails his talent, his destiny and his God.
GEORGE LOIS
*The Art of Advertising*, 1977


Absence of occupation is not rest / A mind quite
vacant is a mind distressed.
WILLIAM COWPER
"Retirement", 1782

Usually, when people are sad, they don't do
anything. They just cry over their condition. But
when they get angry they bring about change.
MALCOLM X<br>
Malcom X Speaks, 1965

Anger represents a certain power when a great
mind, prevented from executing its own generous
desires, is moved by it.
PIETRO ARETINO, 1537

# Work

Work is the only dirty four-letter word in the
language.
ABBIE HOFFMAN, 1970

Most of the world's troubles seem to come from
people who are too busy. If only politicians and
scientists were lazier, how much happier we
should all be. The lazy man is preserved from the
commission of almost all of the nastier crimes and
many of the motives which make us sacrifice to toil
the innocent enjoyment of leisure are amongst the
most ignoble: pride, avarice, emulation, vainglory
and the appetite for power over others.
EVELYN WAUGH, 1962

To do nothing at all is the most difficult thing in
the world, the most difficult and the most
intellectual.
OSCAR WILDE<br>
Intentions, 1891

Men need some kind of external activity, because
they are inactive within.
SCHOPENHAUER
*Parerga and Paralipomena*, 1851


One is always seeking the touchstone that will
dissolve one's deficiencies as a person and a
craftsman. And one is always bumping up against
the fact that there is none except hard work,
concentration and continued application.
PAUL GALLICO
*Confessions of a Story Teller*, 1961


I work so hard to find out what I have to do, not
what I like to do.
MIES VAN DER ROHE, 1963


Determine never to be idle. No person will have
occasion to complain of the want of time who
never loses any. It is wonderful how much may be
done if we are always doing.
THOMAS JEFFERSON, 1787


Our nature consists in motion; complete rest is
death.
PASCAL
*Pensées*, 1670


The majority prove their worth by keeping busy. A
busy life is the nearest thing to a purposeful life.
ERIC HOFFER
*The Ordeal of Change*, 1964


The highest pleasure to be got out of freedom, and
having nothing to do, is labor.
MARK TWAIN, 1876

If thou be not busy for thyself now, who shall be
busy for thee in time to come?
THOMAS À KEMPIS<br>
The Imitation of Christ, 1426

What is worth doing is worth the trouble of asking
somebody to do it.
AMBROSE BIERCE<br>
The Devil's Dictionary, 1881–1911

Work was like cats were supposed to be; if you
disliked and feared it and tried to keep out of its
way, it knew at once and sought you out ...
KINGSLEY AMIS<br>
Take a Girl Like You, 1960

The really efficient laborer will be found not to
crowd his day with work, but will saunter to his
task surrounded by a wide halo of ease and leisure.
THOREAU<br>
Journal, 1841

There is no kind of idleness by which we are so
easily seduced as that which dignifies itself by the
appearance of business.
SAMUEL JOHNSON<br>
The Idler, 1758–60

The ant is knowing and wise; but he doesn't know
enough to take a vacation.
CLARENCE DAY<br>
This Simian World, 1920

To be at ease is better than to be at business.
Nothing really belongs to us but time, which even
he has who has nothing else.
BALTASAR GRACIÁN<br>
The Art of Worldly Wisdom, 1647

It is only by labour that thought can be made
healthy, and only by thought that labour can be
made happy, and the two cannot be separated
with impunity.
RUSKIN
*The Stones of Venice*, 1851–3

Every man's task is his life-preserver.
EMERSON
*The Conduct of Life*, 1860

Let us be grateful to Adam our benefactor. He cut
us out of the "blessing" of idleness and won for us
the "curse" of labor.
MARK TWAIN
*Following the Equator*, 1897

Love labor: for if thou dost not want it for food,
thou mayest for physic. It is wholesome for thy
body and good for thy mind.
WILLIAM PENN
*Some Fruits of Solitude*, 1693

Work spares us from three great evils: boredom,
vice and need.
VOLTAIRE
*Candide*, 1759

It is necessary to work, if not from inclination, at
least from despair. Everything considered, work is
less boring than amusing oneself.
BAUDELAIRE
*Mon coeur mis à nu*, 1887

He who does nothing renders himself incapable of
doing anything; but while we are executing any
work, we are preparing and qualifying ourselves to
undertake another.
WILLIAM HAZLITT

He that can work is a born king of something.
THOMAS CARLYLE
*Chartism*, 1839

Work is a dull thing; you cannot get away from
that. The only agreeable existence is one of
idleness, and that is not, unfortunately, always
compatible with continuing to exist at all.

ROSE MACAULAY

The life of labor does not make men, but drudges.

EMERSON<br>
Journals, 1843

One of the saddest things is that the only thing a
man can do for eight hours a day, day after day, is
work. you can't eat eight hours a day nor drink for
eight hours a day nor make love for eight hours.

WILLIAM FAULKNER, 1958

I like work: it fascinates me. I can sit and look at it
for hours. I love to keep it by me: the idea of getting
rid of it nearly breaks my heart.

JEROME K. JEROME<br>
Three Men In A Boat, 1889

Most people work the greater part of their time for
a mere living; and the little freedom which
remains to them so troubles them that they use
every means of getting rid of it.

GOETHE<br>
The Sorrows of Young Werther, 1774

I love idleness so much and so dearly, that I have
hardly the heart to say a word against it . . .

CHARLES JAMES FOX

All paid employments absorb and degrade the
mind.

ARISTOTLE, 384–322 B.C.

When work is a pleasure, life is a joy! When work
is a duty, life is slavery.

MAXIM GORKY<br>
The Lower Depths, 1903

People say that life is the thing, but I prefer
reading.
LOGAN PEARSALL SMITH
*Trivia*, 1917

Style and structure are the essence of a book; great
ideas are hogwash.
VLADIMIR NABOKOV, 1958

The writer is the Faust of modern society, the only
surviving individualist in a mass age. To his
orthodox contemporaries he seems a semi-
madman.
BORIS PASTERNAK, 1959

... better far write twaddle or anything, anything
than nothing at all.
KATHERINE MANSFIELD
*Journal*, 1922

It is the writer's privilege to help man endure by
lifting his heart.
WILLIAM FAULKNER

Writing is not a profession but a vocation of
unhappiness. I don't think an artist can ever be
happy.
GEORGES SIMENON, 1958

An author ought to write for the youth of his own
generation, the critics of the next, and the
schoolmasters of ever afterwards.
F. SCOTT FITZGERALD

Of making many books there is no end, and much
study is a weariness of the flesh.
Ecclesiastes 12:12

A book is only your point of view.
KATHERINE HEPBURN, 1967

Get stewed: / Books are a load of crap.

PHILIP LARKIN
"A Study of Reading Habits", *The Whitsun
Weddings*, 1964

Technique alone is never enough. You have to
have passion. Technique alone is just an
embroidered potboiler.

RAYMOND CHANDLER
*Notebooks of Raymond Chandler*, 1977

That's what a writer is – an ordinary guy who
happens to write well.

JOHN O'HARA, 1969

A great many people now reading and writing
would be better employed in keeping rabbits.

EDITH SITWELL, 1923

All writing is garbage. People who come out of
nowhere to try to put into words any part of what
goes on in their minds are pigs.

ANTONIN ARTAUD
*Selected Writings*, 1976

Writing is a cop-out. An excuse to live perpetually
in fantasy land, where you can create, direct and
watch the products of your own head. Very selfish.

MONICA DICKENS, 1976

Sir, no man but a blockhead ever wrote, except for
money.

SAMUEL JOHNSON
in Boswell, *Life of Johnson*, 1791

What is literature compared with cooking? The
one is shadow, the other substance.

E. V. LUCAS

It is not a writer's business to hold opinions.

W. B. YEATS

## *(Entries in bold denotes topics covered)*